Margaret Feinberg is a prophetic voice to our generation. This book will pierce your soul and create a renewed hunger to seek God.

> MARK BATTERSON, pastor of National Community Church and author of *In a Pit with a Lion on a Snowy Day*

Margaret challenges and reminds us what it truly means to long for God and to really know him. As leaders, we need to be reminded of this, and Margaret hits the target. She's one of the authentic and vital voices for our generation.

> BRAD LOMENICK, executive director of Catalyst

Margaret Feinberg's *Hungry for God* will help you hear God's voice in your everyday life. It is wonderfully prayerful and practical, touching on subjects such as the importance of quality Kairos Moments with God and the diversity of the languages in which he may choose to speak to us. Margaret's usual engaging style combines personal stories with biblical truths and gives practical steps in learning to hear the Father's still, small voice in all its many guises. I recommend this book wholeheartedly to anyone seeking to develop and maintain a healthy spiritual appetite.

> PETE GREIG, director of prayer for Alpha International, cofounder of 24–7 Prayer, and author of *Red Moon Rising* and *God on Mute*

Reading *Hungry for God* is a celebration—engaging my soul and spirit to God's heart through powerfully deep and challenging words from my new friend, Margaret. For you, the reader, this could be an embracing of daily moments, listening to and hearing "the whisper of God."

ESTHER BURROUGHS, author, speaker, and founder of Treasures of the Heart Ministry

Once again, in Margaret Feinberg-style, we see a refreshing look at recognizing God's voice in our everyday life. And we are challenged to act on what we hear. Thank you, Margaret, for your own hunger for God and for sharing your journey with us. You always make us hungrier for him as well!

CHRIS ADAMS, senior lead women's ministry specialist

With the candor of a child and the vision of an artist, Margaret Feinberg paints fresh pictures, opening windows so that I can better see, taste, and know the Lover of my soul.

DEE BRESTIN, author of *The God of All Comfort*

In *Hungry for God*, Margaret Feinberg whets our appetites for the full feast God has prepared for us. Pull up a chair, pick up a fork, and dive in!

ELISA MORGAN, president of Mission: Momentum and author of *She Did What She Could*

hungry for
GOD

Also by Margaret Feinberg

The Organic God

The Sacred Echo

Scouting the Divine

*Each book is also available
as part of a six-week DVD Bible study
at www.margaretfeinberg.com.

Margaret Feinberg

hungry for
GOD

Hearing God's voice in the ordinary and the everyday

ZONDERVAN®

ZONDERVAN.com/
AUTHORTRACKER
follow your favorite authors

ZONDERVAN

Hungry for God
Copyright © 2011 by Margaret Feinberg

This title is also available as a Zondervan ebook.
Visit www.zondervan.com/ebooks.

This title is also available in a Zondervan audio edition.
Visit www.zondervan.fm.

Requests for information should be addressed to:
Zondervan, *Grand Rapids, Michigan* 49530

Library of Congress Cataloging-in-Publication Data

Feinberg, Margaret, 1976-
      Hungry for God : hearing God's voice in the ordinary and the everyday /
Margaret Feinberg.
            p.   cm.
      ISBN 978-0-310-33207-7 (softcover)
      1. Christian life. 2. Spiritual life — Christianity. 3. Listening — Religious aspects
— Christianity. I. Title.
      BV4501.3.F455   2011
      248.4 — dc22   2011006754

Published in association with Yates & Yates, www.yates2.com.

Cover design: Kelly Michael Johnson
Cover photography: Audrey Brooks
Interior design: Beth Shagene

Printed in the United States of America

11 12 13 14 15 16 /QG/ 21 20 19 18 17 16 15 14 13 12 11 10 9 8 7 6 5 4 3 2 1

Contents

Hidden Bonus Tracks

Earth's crammed with heaven
And every common bush afire with God:
But only he who sees, takes off his shoes.

Elizabeth Barrett Browning

Divine Appetite

For three days no grilled skirt steak, fresh guacamole, homemade salsa, or slices of lime. Instead I ask God a question:

What does it mean to hunger for you?

My stomach mumbles and grumbles, refusing to let me forget that I haven't eaten solid food for nearly seventy-two hours. The sacrifice hasn't been easy. Some people need to remind themselves to eat; I have to remind myself to stop eating. I count Rachael, Paula, and Emeril from the Food Network as friends, and *Iron Chef* among my favorite shows.

Though fasts have always been difficult for me, this one has been especially laborious. The first day I had sharp pains and constant discomfort. My mind was foggy, my responsiveness slow. Worse, anyone unlucky enough to stray into my path became a target for grumpiness. The second day, the condition of my body, mind, and temperament was slightly improved—though everyone I encountered was still fair game.

Today is different. I've made peace with the hollow

companion in my stomach, the sudden twinges of belly pain replaced by a dull ache. While I'm still grumpy, I hold my tongue: it's me, not you.

With the discomfort subsiding, I've welcomed a sense of clarity. Colors are more vibrant, details more refined. Thoughts meander rather than scamper away. Reflecting on God and offering up a prayer feels natural, almost effortless.

Why don't I fast more often? I wonder. Then I remember the first two days, and how much I miss my foodie friends.

I don't know anything about real hunger. While billions suffer in starvation and poverty, I live behind the plush curtain. Yet hunger is woven into the fabric of our humanness—no matter where we live. Appetite is a primitive desire that doesn't discriminate; every human has felt its pangs. Without an appetite, we slip into starvation and even death. Hunger is the gnawing reminder that in order to have strength, we must have sustenance.

As I've thought and prayed during this time, I've wondered if the ache I feel inside parallels what it means to have a divine appetite for God. If physical hunger is a set of feelings that leads a person to search for food, then spiritual hunger is a set of experiences and longings that compels a person to search for God. Just as my body needs food to survive, my spirit needs God to thrive. A divine appetite drives me to pursue a vibrant relationship with God—one in which I find my sustenance and strength.

Our spiritual appetites can be quelled only by God. But is it possible to dine on an intangible being? How do we feast upon something we cannot see, touch, or taste? Over the last several years, I've learned that God's voice is the only entrée that can nourish our ethereal cravings. Hearing and experiencing, rather than eating, assuages spiritual hunger.

My spiritual hunger grumbles loudest when I feel furthest from God. Though I cling to the assertion that God is everywhere and promises to never leave or forsake us, I've spent days, weeks, even months wondering, *Are you there God? It's me, Margaret.*

I long for a single word to appease my spiritual belly. When the silence finally breaks, the sound of God's voice is a banquet for my soul—every syllable a tasty morsel, every expression flavored with love.

Longing to know him.

Longing to experience him.

Longing to hear him.

Is that what it means to hunger for God?

These are some of the foundational longings of my heart, but like most I've tried to satiate the desire for God by stuffing myself with carbohydrates and comfort, entertainment and distraction, activity and productivity —anything to fill the void. A thousand times over I've discovered that these things don't satisfy.

Maybe that's why I keep returning to this issue of hungering for God. More than a decade ago, a friend gave me the opportunity to publish my first book. Though I considered submitting a dozen different ideas, I decided to explore what it looks like to pursue God and hear his voice. In some ways, I've never stopped mining these themes, as evidenced in *The Organic God*, *The Sacred Echo*, and *Scouting the Divine*. I hope I never do.

I wrote *God Whispers: Learning to Hear His Voice* exploring the belief that as followers of Jesus, we are wired to hear and respond to the voice of God in our lives. Instead of shouting, God takes a subtle, gentle approach to communicating with us. Instead of filling the solar system with Star Wars presentations, carving words in tree bark, or dropping parchment from the sky, God whispers in order to draw us closer. While God can reveal himself through a trumpeting angel descending from the sky, the presence of the divine often greets us in the mundane, in the midst of our workday routines and everyday circumstances.

I've continued to grow spiritually since *God Whispers* first released a decade ago. This updated version has been revised and retitled to reflect this growth. One thing that hasn't changed is my hunger for a vibrant relationship with God—one in which I not only know that he hears my voice, but I also hear his. It's the kind of relationship in which we're growing in intimate knowledge of each other (though God obviously has a head start on that one), and delight in one another each day.

Learning to hear God's voice is more like enjoying a good book than completing a doctorate; it's more like mastering an instrument than achieving an award—in other words, you never quit growing and discovering. My hope and prayer is that God's voice will become a natural melody in the music of your life, such that he becomes the highlight of your every day.

May the hunger for God stir in your heart.

Blessings,
Margaret

.001 An Unforgettable Invitation

As a child I climbed out of bed early each morning, walked into the living room in footie pajamas, and encountered a familiar scene: my mom sitting on the couch reading her Bible. The image is one of my fondest childhood memories. Though my parents taught me countless lessons about God while I was growing up, the sight of my mom perched on the sofa searching the Scriptures was the most powerful. Each morning as she studied and prayed, she gave me a portrait of what it looks like to forage for the divine.

Both of my parents taught me what it means to turn life's routines into adventures and how to keep one's ears attuned to God along the way. Free spirits who embarked on new undertakings every few years, my parents went from manufacturing surfboards in Florida to building their own end-of-the-world home in North Carolina to living as ski bums for a winter in Colorado—never shying away from new exploits. Because they weren't attached to a particular denomination, we attended a different type of church wherever we lived. At each new place of worship, I always liked asking the people we met a question: *How do you hear from God?*

The answers were as diverse as the people I asked, and most answers left me more confused. Some didn't seem to worry all that much about hearing from God. One pastor told me, "You just know deep down inside."

"But *how* do you know?" I'd protest.

Others relied on spiritual language. One bubbly churchgoing woman described having something she called a "check in her spirit." Still others claimed to hear from God all day every day, as if they had a Commissioner Gordon–style red phone at home with a direct connection to God's heavenly secretary. These people scared me.

When I asked my mom about hearing from God, she used much of the same language as everyone else. I knew *her* words were genuine; but still what she said didn't compute. None of it was getting through my overly inquisitive ten-year-old skull, and Mom could tell. That's when she decided to try something different. We prayed together, asking God to speak and reveal himself to me.

I had no idea such a simple prayer could be so powerful.

God Sings

One Sunday, the children's lesson was on how the name of Jesus has power and authority. That night I dreamt I was cornered on the edge of a steep, rugged cliff by a pack of wolves. The ravenous animals snarled; their sharp ivory teeth snapped. If I didn't do something, I would be torn apart. I remembered the words of my Sunday school teacher and cried out, "In the name of Jesus, go away." Like a hand, an invisible sweeping motion shoved the wolves over the side of the cliff. Then I woke up.

God turned a simple dream into a concert hall where he could sing about the power of his Son's name. The experience taught me that God was real, active, and engaged in my life, and I didn't need to ascend a magical mountaintop to meet with him. The dream stirred my hunger to know God more and illustrated just how personal God is when it comes to speaking to us. Not only am I a visual learner, but I'm also a visual communicator. God knew this, and in his love used the images of dreams to make himself real to me.

As I grew older, God continued to answer my mother's prayer by expanding my understanding of the ways in which he speaks. God would make a Scripture come alive in my heart and imagination—causing a story or passage to grab my attention like a colorful billboard on a desolate highway. God used everything from interactions with nature to experiences in everyday life to speak to me. Sometimes conversations with a friend rang in my spirit, or I'd hear a sermon with an unforgettable refrain.

As a teenager, I often struggled with the awkwardness
that accompanies adolescence both in my personal life and
in my relationship with God. My first semester at college,
I attended too many parties, kissed too many boys, and
drank too much cheap beer. Everyone kept telling me
that these were supposed to be the best years of my life,
so I wondered why I felt so empty and my relationships
so hollow. My best party friends on Friday night didn't
remember my name on sober Monday. Something needed
to change.

My first summer of college, I attended a Christian
conference in Colorado. As I listened to the speakers, I felt
the hunger stirring in my heart. I was away from God and
miserable. I laid my face in my Bible and cried out, asking
God to become the center and focus of my life again. Calm
enveloped me. In the stillness of my being, the following
words ran through my mind: *You are my child, and I love you.
You are mine; you are not your own. Come back to me.*

God grabbed me by the scruff of the neck. As God's child,
wholly loved, I found myself running back to Jesus again.
Like a kitten flopping as its mother carries it to a safe place,
I let myself dangle in God's gentle grip—and experienced
new depths of peace. The faith my parents had exposed me
to growing up became my own. God was still answering
my mother's prayer.

I returned to college with the same haircut and student ID number, but everything else changed. The hunger for God returned to my life. Reading the Bible became such a delight that I became a religion major, focusing on New Testament studies. I also made a sincere effort to attend the campus-based ministries. Looking back, I realize that many of the students who attended these events were still wrestling to make the faith they had grown up with their own. While they engaged in all-night discussions on predestination versus free will, I found myself wondering about all of the young women in my sorority who didn't know Jesus yet. Recognizing that I was one of the few followers of Jesus among this group of women, I decided we needed more believers. I prayed that during the upcoming rush, a two-week period in which we accepted new members, forty would be followers of Jesus. Since we were taking only sixty total, my friends thought I was crazy. They could understand falling to their knees before God during climactic situations, like a depressing diagnosis or game-changing job offer; but asking God to engage in a silly sorority didn't strike them as a good use of God's time. One well-meaning Christian friend challenged me, "Aren't you being selfish? If you ask for forty Christians, then none of the other sororities will get any."

I didn't care. I prayed anyway. And when rush concluded, forty of the new members *were* followers of Jesus. The experience taught me the power and potential of prayer and gave me the courage to make seemingly outlandish requests of God. I had begun listening and looking for God, and he continued to sing over me.

Though my faith was coming alive, I made countless mistakes during those years. Sometimes I tried too hard to convince someone of their need for God, and pushed them farther away. Other times I was afraid to speak up. My theology wobbly, my heart filled with pride, my hypocrisy often undermined anything I tried to communicate.

Yet I was growing in my faith, recognizing the importance of reading the Bible, and finding God's voice in my life—if I was willing to listen.

One issue God seemed to be silent on was what I should do after college graduation. I struggled with why God didn't seem to be providing any guidance or direction—worrying that maybe he did, and I missed it. Without an inkling, I filled out applications and collected rejection slips. From the few positive responses, I accepted an internship at a magazine I'd never heard of before in Lake Mary, Florida. I spent the summer learning about publishing and stumbled into a career of writing and communicating, a career which, looking back, God had designed me for.

You are mine; you are not your own still resonates in my being

years after that Christian conference I attended in college.
The words were a turning point in my life. One of the
mysteries and marvels of the divine is that we never know
when God will speak or how the words will transform our
lives forever.

Hearing from God is foundational to a vibrant spiritual
relationship with him. We're created with the capacity
to know what brings God delight and to recognize his
involvement in our lives. We're meant to discover God's
passions, pleasures, and pains, designed to recognize his
voice and its inflections. I don't know if my mom had these
things in mind when she prayed for me years ago, but I still
feel the ripples of her divine request.

God Beckons

God's voice always contains an invitation to know him
more, and the process of listening for God beckons us
to grow in our knowledge of both the temporal and the
transcendent.

Such is the lesson in 1 Kings 18–19 when Elijah answers
the invitation to follow and know God with abandon.
Given a "mission: impossible" by God, Elijah is instructed
to speak out against the false prophets and wicked leaders
ruling over the land. His decision to obey leads to a fiery
showdown on top of Mount Carmel in which the false

prophets are defeated and Elijah becomes the target of the wicked leaders' scorn. He escapes with his life, but falls into deep depression. He begs God to let him die. God refuses. Though Elijah doesn't feel particularly hungry for God, his body cries out for food. Twice God sends an angel to feed Elijah, and, strengthened by the meal, Elijah travels to Mount Horeb.

Horeb—a name used by some biblical writers to refer to the Sinai region—is, in the Hebrew Scriptures, one of God's favorite places to offer invitations. Here God calls Moses and invites the Israelites into a divine covenant. At Horeb the Israelites accept God's invitation to travel to Canaan and Kadesh-Barnea. It's no surprise, then, that God meets Elijah in this special place to invite the prophet into a deeper relationship.

Elijah is just coming off the crowning achievement of his career: God was faithful to honor his every request as he defeated the false prophets at Carmel. But Queen Jezebel decides to rain on his party. She places a price on his head and promises to have him killed.

"How could this be, God?" Elijah must have wondered. "Did you give me victory only to allow defeat?"

Emotionally drained, the depressed prophet shuffles into a cave on the side of the mountain. He's physically spent. In the midst of the wilderness of silence, God calls Elijah by name, asking, "What are you doing here?"

The prophet rips into God, alleging that his fervent dedication and willingness to risk everything has been in vain. The Israelites have rejected God, destroyed the holy places, and killed the true prophets anyway. With a bounty on his head, Elijah has nowhere to go.

God doesn't address a single one of Elijah's allegations; but he does respond. He instructs Elijah to stand on the side of the mountain and wait for his passing.

Elijah obeys.

The prophet feels a breeze. A gust of wind lifts his hair in all directions. He brushes a handful out of his eyes before scrambling inside the mouth of the cave. A thunderous wind shatters the mountainside, scattering rocks in all directions. Despite its power and ferocity, God is not in that wind.

Hesitant to step outside the cave, Elijah feels the ground vibrate beneath him. He loses his footing and falls to the ground as the earth convulses. Still regaining his composure, he squints when a shaft of fire descends from the sky and a wave of heat blasts across his face. Smoke fills his nostrils. Elijah wonders what's next. A lightning bolt? A volcanic eruption? A flood?

He waits. Finally he hears a thin silence like a gentle whisper. Elijah knows the presence and recognizes the voice. He stands up, dusts himself off, and pulls his coat over his face.

Approaching the opening of the cave, God calls Elijah by name and asks the prophet a second time, "What are you doing here?" Elijah offers God the exact same answer as before, as if God hadn't heard him the first time. Only now does God answer Elijah's concerns with specific directives reminding him that he is not the last prophet — seven thousand others refuse to bow their knees to Baal.

As with Job, God doesn't give Elijah a full explanation and grant him understanding. Instead God offers and reveals himself. As Elijah is sitting in a musty cave in the midst of a Middle Eastern mountain range, God makes contact with the prophet. Rather than manifest himself in all his brilliant glory and splendid power, God chooses to whisper.

The image of a whisper speaks to the posture of our relationship with God. Whispering is ineffective if the person we're trying to communicate with is on the other side of the room. God doesn't desire a long-distance relationship, but an intimate one. Though the clamor of the wind, earthquake, and fire garner Elijah's attention, the stillness of the whisper grabs his heart and brings him to a place where he is able to receive God's answer.

Elijah's story demonstrates God's ability to speak into any situation. No matter the darkness I might be in, God has a way of bringing me to a place where I can encounter him. Like Elijah's, my pilgrimage is often difficult, riddled with silence and self-doubt. Like Elijah, I don't always get the answer that I want, but the one I need.

I've wrestled with God over the issue of my health. I've experienced days when I've wanted to call it quits. Over the last five years I've visited countless doctors to try to find a diagnosis and remedy for a stomach illness, which often leaves me fatigued, writhing in pain, and unable to keep food down. Even after eliminating wheat and full-fat dairy from my diet, and adding a regimen of drugs and vitamins, all too often I still find myself in bed with nausea and stomach cramps. Looking at my travel bag of prescription medicine, I feel like a walking pharmacy. I joke that my medicine cabinet could become our retirement plan.

Just this morning, I became ill after eating an apple. My body rejected the food. I feel the raw sting in the back of my throat. On this day, as on hundreds of others, I've asked God for healing and restoration. I've also wrestled God through questions like, *Why? Why do you allow this? Why don't you heal?* I know nothing is impossible for God. The Gospels are littered with stories of healing, and I'm begging for the scraps. Despite thousands of prayers, I squat in the silence longing for a healing that I have not yet laid hold of.

I often think of Paul, who pleads for God to remove the thorn in his side. Some scholars believe the thorn is a metaphor for a physical malady. Whatever form the thorn took, God refuses to remove it, reminding Paul that divine grace is sufficient. The experience must have challenged Paul's relationship with God. The malady kept him pleading, and yet the experience also taught him to trust God in his own discomfort.

My experiences with illness challenge me in my relationship with God. The illness makes me feel what it's like to hunger and ache and not be able to find relief in anything but God. Will I still wait on God? Will I trust God in the discomfort?

As I listen for God in the midst of silence and hardship, I must decide whether I'm willing to give up listening for what I want to hear and begin listening to what God is actually saying. This decision applies not only to healing, but to all of the issues I lay before God. As with Elijah on the mountainside, God doesn't answer my concerns directly but reveals something else. I've sought God on issues of dealing with a difficult person, only to find my own sour attitude spotlighted. I've asked for clarity on the future, only to discover God's in the process of strengthening my faith.

I've begged for an escape from a heated situation, only to discover that God planted me in a greenhouse of growth.

Asking God to speak means we must come to him on his terms, not our own. Too often we look for God in the earthquakes and windstorms when God has been whispering into our lives all along. We'd do well to quit waiting for lightning to strike and instead start looking for God now. When we start recognizing and feasting on God's words in the everyday, life becomes grander.

As we set out on this journey together, I pray for you what my mother prayed for me as child:

I ask that you would experience the voice and presence of God. I ask that God give you eyes to see the ways in which he is moving in your life, ears to hear his voice, and a heart that beats passionately after the Divine. I pray you will answer the invitation to know God, recognize his voice, and become an example of what it looks like to live with reckless abandon for Christ. Amen.

.002 Kairos Moments

I awaken before my alarm. The moment the sun sneaks around the edges of the curtains, sleep escapes me. I roll out of bed, grab my Bible, and nestle under a down blanket in the corner of the couch. Still half asleep, I flip open the Scriptures and begin reading wherever it topples open. The first verse slaps me cold across the face: "This they will have in return for their pride, because they have taunted and become arrogant against the people of the Lord of hosts" (Zephaniah 2:10).

That's what I get for playing Bible roulette. I should have known better. After all, the corner of the page boasted the author's name: Zephaniah. Old Testament prophets are high-risk for unfortunate verses.

Lord, are you speaking to me?

A woman I serve alongside at a local ministry comes to mind. Seeing her name on the schedule always makes me grimace. On joint projects, she bats ideas down like furry gophers in a traveling carnival game, her stern face only fueling my irritation. Driving away from a recent meeting together, I drew an unkind caricature of her in my mind. I shared my frustration with my husband and vented about her with a friend the next day.

I read the verse again.

> *For their pride.*
> *Taunted and become arrogant.*
> *Against the people of the Lord.*

The phrases describe my experience, and the Scriptures describe me. Though I've been quick to point fingers at the woman, I'm the proud and arrogant one. I've assumed that I knew better—never bothering to dig deeper into this woman's story or background. I didn't want to resolve our differences as much as I wanted to refute her.

Father, forgive me. Don't let my arrogance stamp out my hunger for you. Change me, transform my heart. Help me to be a source of reconciliation and resolution. Amen.

The first gentle wave of peace I've experienced since the meeting floods my heart. My attitude shifts, reorienting my heart toward the woman and God. I look at the clock. Only ten minutes have passed since I woke up. I've encountered a Kairos Moment.

A Different Kind of Time

The ancient Greeks both measured and celebrated time. Maybe that's one reason the Scripture uses two different

Greek words for time. The first, *chronos*, expresses time in measurable units: seasons, dates, calendars, and clocks. *Chronos* points to the before and the after; this kind of time is counted, marked off, measured with precision. Westerners like talking in *chronos* terms. Our standards of minutes, hours, days, and weeks keep score of the chronological passing of time.

But the Greeks regard time as more than a measurement; it's also a gift to be savored and experienced. Perhaps that's why they have a second word for time, *kairos*, which looks beyond the measurement of time and into its potential. *Chronos* is concerned with quantity; *kairos* asks us to consider quality, invites us to recognize and seize the divine, opportune moments before us.

When God speaks into our lives, the *kairos* interrupts the *chronos*. I call these experiences Kairos Moments, and they carry the potential to reorient our lives. They challenge our attitudes and invite repentance. They steady our steps when the footing of life seems unstable, shine a light when the path grows dim, and remind us we are not alone, even when no other soul seems to understand.

The problem is that hunger tends to force *chronos* thinking. We're watching the clock, wondering *when* God will speak. Instead, we should recognize that God is speaking right now, and we should be asking *how* he wants to talk to us.

Kairos Moments are like a dinner bell for the spiritually starved. Recognizing these moments gets us to stop and listen, knowing God is about to rock our world.

The Scriptures are laced with these occasions. God formed the world with his voice. Behind all the wonders in nature is the spoken word. God's presence. Though many focus on *chronos* in the first two chapters of Genesis, the story of God in creation is illuminated by the *kairos*. Brightness filling the expanse. Land forming. Oceans splashing to life.

In the opening scenes of Genesis, we catch a glimpse of Adam and Eve walking in communion with God. Genesis never reveals the length of time Adam and Eve enjoy their garden relationship with God; the story isn't as concerned with the *chronos* as with the *kairos*. When sin enters the world through a willful act of disobedience, perfect communion between God and humanity shatters. Yet God doesn't lose his voice after the original sin. If anything, he finds it—the first recorded dialogue with God occurs *after* the fruit is consumed.

Adam and Eve lose access to the garden, but they never lose God. One of God's first acts after the fall is to make them designer animal skin clothing. When the couple steps across Eden's boundary, they don't travel naked or alone. God goes with them, and continues to speak.

The Scriptures are threaded with individuals who hear God's voice. He doesn't just speak to Adam and Eve, but goes on to speak to their children, grandchildren, and great-grandchildren throughout the ages. God speaks to Cain, Noah, Abram, and Hagar. First Samuel 3:4 records the Lord's call to Samuel as a young boy, to which Samuel responds, "Here I am." This response launches Samuel into a remarkable life story of serving and obeying God. We don't know how long each of these encounters lasts, but we know their significance well—and that's the mark of a Kairos Moment.

Consider Hebrews 11, often referred to as the "Hall of Faith" chapter of the Bible. Here, the author lists numerous exemplars of faith from the Hebrew Scriptures, many of whom hear from God. Not only does God speak to and through people; he also appears to them. Abram, Isaac, and Solomon all have visual encounters with God. The voice that echoes in the Old Testament is heard throughout the New. With water beads slipping down Jesus' face after baptism, an audible voice declares, "This is My beloved Son, in whom I am well-pleased." The words of that Kairos Moment mark Jesus' ministry forever.

Even after the death and resurrection of Jesus, God continues to speak publicly and even audibly to humanity. Saul and his travel companions encounter God's voice in a profound Kairos Moment when a voice asks, "Saul, Saul, why do you persecute me?" This one question changes the life of Saul and the history of the church forever.

God's speaking to us is not bound by *chronos*. The divine pace and timing are different from ours. As he does with Saul, God surprises us with his voice and presence. These Kairos Moments beckon us into a deeper relationship with God and stir up our hunger to know God. This morning's Scripture uncovered the ugly attitude of pride and arrogance in my heart and invited me to change, to realign my heart with God's. What will tomorrow bring?

A Much-Needed Voice

Kairos Moments remind me of how much I need God's steady presence and guidance in my life. I make decisions based on what I hear and know. If I'm not hearing from God and recognizing his presence, then I have to wonder what I'm basing my decisions on. Tossed to and fro by dozens of opportunities, ideas, dreams, and closed doors, I realize how much I need God to navigate the maze of everyday life.

I've found great comfort in Isaiah 30:21, which promises, "Your ears will hear a word behind you, 'This is the way, walk in it,' whenever you turn to the right or to the left." Our spiritual stomachs are ever growling, but God is always feeding us. Whenever I read this passage, I imagine God's Spirit behind me, whispering, "A little to the left, Margaret, now a little to the right." God often takes years to position us in the place he has in mind, rarely revealing the entire plan at one time. The Lord nudges and leads a half step here, a quarter step there, to get us where he wants us to go.

My internship after college graduation was not the one I wanted. I wanted to intern for a magazine called *Charisma*. When the editor left a message on my answering machine, I was thrilled, but when I called him back, he said that *Charisma's* internship had been filled. If I was available, though, another of the company's magazines needed an intern. I'd never heard of *Christian Retailing*, so the editor explained that the magazine went to Christian bookstore owners to inform them of new products and trends within the Christian publishing industry. Disappointed, I nonetheless accepted the offer.

Only years later, did I realize the significance of that moment. If I had been given the *Charisma* internship, I would have learned about working at a magazine, but by accepting the position at *Christian Retailing*, I learned the intricate details of the publishing world and valuable insights that prepared me for what I do today. When the editor called, I felt thrown by God, but now I look back and recognize the wisdom and grace of God's guidance. A job that seemed undesirable at first was a custom-embossed invitation to prepare me for the work God was calling me to do.

Elijah is a prophet known for his many Kairos Moments with God, as he discovers early in his ministry. In 1 Kings 17 and 18, he is directed and redirected by the Lord three times. He is sent to a ravine east of the Jordan, where he drinks from a brook and is fed by ravens. When the brook dries up, the Lord sends Elijah to live with a widow at Zarephath. Then he is sent to the evil king Ahab, where, as we've seen, he defeats the followers of Baal.

What if Elijah had never made it past that brook? What if he followed the first set of instructions but refused the next? Elijah recognized that following God is a pilgrimage marked by long tunnels, sudden turns, and unexpected encounters. He pursued God through valleys and across mountains until he arrived at his destination, a life of glorifying the Lord.

A Transformative Story

Kairos Moments are some of my most precious treasures. As followers of Jesus, we have the opportunity to fill our own spiritual vaults with lasting treasures — the Words of the King. Words that breathe life, deliver hope. When God speaks into our lives, the stories of transformation not only fuel our own faith but also the faith of those around us. We are given the opportunity to record these moments in journals and online, use them in life lessons, and lock them deep within our hearts where the pages won't tear or soil.

Years ago I heard a woman describe an image she saw in her mind, in which the Lord asked her to travel down a road. She obeyed until she came upon a red panel that blocked the road and reached into the sky. She touched it. Soft like fabric, the red covering hid a wall that felt impenetrable. She cried out to God because she could find no way around, and he said, *Let me show you my perspective.*

The woman was given a bird's-eye view of the scene: the roadblock was a ribbon wrapping a huge present with a bow on top. What once appeared as a barrier transformed into an enormous gift, all because of a shift in perspective.

After this woman shared her Kairos Moment, I felt like it became mine. The image has come to mind dozens of times over the years. In moments when the doors of opportunity slam shut and channels of provision run dry, I'm reminded that even dead ends can become an unexpected gift from God.

Sometimes a Kairos Moment is the only thing that gives me the courage to keep going. I know I'm not alone. A Kairos

Moment gave Abraham's wife, Sarah, the promise of a
child when all hope was long gone. A Kairos Moment gave
Noah the courage to build a boat to save his family, and
strengthened Joseph's faith even when he found himself
wrongly imprisoned. Did God speak to these men and
women of faith for a few seconds or many hours? We don't
know. But the message was powerful.

My friend's father was a private pilot. Once, out on a lone
flight, his plane disappeared off the radar. The news swept
through the community. Search parties were sent out by
ground and air; nighttime vigils were organized. My friend
and her family clung on to hope that they'd find him, but
the days rolled into weeks, then months. Though my friend
wasn't religious, I prayed for and with her.

Before her father had left for the airport, they'd had a
wicked argument, and now she begged for the chance to
make things right. I prayed, asking God to protect and save
her dad—to do something, anything—and in a Kairos
Moment, I sensed that God wanted me to *be with her,*
above all else. Everyone knew that the more *chronos* that
passed, the less likely it was that he had survived, but she
and I never gave voice to that fear. Instead, we discussed
anything and everything else, then sat in silence together.
We took long drives and hung out in parks. Somehow she
survived through the painful season of not knowing, until

the dreaded news arrived: they found the plane and his body.

That was nearly twenty years ago, but my friend still wrestles with the aftermath — unanswered questions, unforgettable regret. To this day I'm still reminded to *be with her*. I call her every few months. When I went more than a year without receiving a returned call, I kept calling. I won't let go of her as a friend. I keep reaching out because the words spoken in that situation are still with me. Though she hasn't met Jesus yet, I continue to pray and wait.

Kairos Moments call us to do things and be people we would not otherwise do and be. They mark our lives by changing our perspective. Though I long for fireworks displays of God's power and thunderous demonstrations of his presence, Kairos Moments often appear in the mundane details of everyday life. Jesus used our hair to remind us of God's intimate knowledge of us, the lilies of the field to teach of provision, and the birds of the air to instruct us in his love.

A Communicating God

Water is one of our most basic needs, yet God uses it to communicate profound truths about himself and his work in our lives. The Scriptures are saturated with meaningful references to water. In the beginning, the Spirit hovers over the water, and during creation, the waters are both separated and gathered. Noah and Moses both float on water as part of their rescue, and the Israelites pass through it when they cross the Red Sea. Prophets pray for rain or against it. Water is used in ritual cleansing, bathing, and baptism. We are promised that water will be part of heaven, too. When I pour a glass of water and sip its refreshing coolness, all of these realities are waiting to be remembered.

If God is willing to use something as basic as water to get our attention, what else might he use? A few years ago, my husband Leif (pronounced Lay-f) and I adopted a little puppy. As soon as the soft brown ball of fur crawled into the palms of my hands, I was in love. We named him Hershey.

After extensive training, Hershey was ready to go anywhere and everywhere. If dogs earned airline status, he'd be triple platinum. Though it sounds silly, sometimes God uses Hershey to teach me spiritual lessons. My furry friend is a living, breathing example of unconditional loyalty and love.

Because Hershey weighs less than five pounds, I carry him with me rather than use a leash. When Hershey stands still and trusts me, I scoop him up in a single motion. But sometimes he thinks I need his help. As I'm leaning down, he'll try to jump up, creating a klutzy moment in which I have to scramble so he doesn't fall. In the split second I'm trying to grab hold of my dog, I've sensed the Holy Spirit whispering, *You do this sometimes too.*

Like Hershey, I don't always trust my master. I think he needs my help. When I jump to take matters into my own hands, rather than trust God, I find everything falling apart. God is faithful and gracious enough to prevent me from thumping on the ground, but these moments remind me of the importance of relying and waiting on him.

Sometimes I wonder if many of us who are hungry for God become distracted by tracking the *chronos,* waiting for God to jump out and start shouting. All the while we are passing by fistfuls of Kairos Moments, pulsating unexpectedly in life's routines. Maybe that's one reason I keep rolling out of bed, reaching for my Bible, and spending time with God. Though I never know when a Kairos Moment will occur, I need to be ready to recognize it—even in the wee hours of the morning, among Hebrew prophets.

.003 Shaped by God's Voice

I'm always amazed at the ways God can use someone else's story to shape us. Years ago I read a story by Jim Cymbala that affected the way I thought about those in need. After the final service one Easter Sunday, the pastor of the famed Brooklyn Tabernacle in New York City felt exhausted. He took a seat on the edge of the platform. When he looked up, a man with matted hair and ragged clothing was walking toward him. As he drew closer, the homeless man offered a crooked grin, revealing two missing front teeth. And his smell—alcohol, sweat, urine, and garbage—took Jim's breath away. Though Jim had worked with the homeless countless times before, this stench was worse than anything he'd ever encountered. Instinct compelled him to turn his head sideways and inhale before looking the man in the eyes.

Jim asked the man his story. David shared that he'd been living in an abandoned truck for the last six years. Jim knew where the story was heading, and reached for the money clip in his back pocket.

The man protested the offer; he didn't want any money.

He wanted Jesus. Jim describes closing his eyes, asking for God's forgiveness. He felt soiled and cheap. Though Jim was a pastor, he'd wanted to get rid of the homeless man as fast as possible, this precious individual crying out for a relationship with Christ—the Savior whose good news Jim had preached all day.

The man buried his filthy face in Jim's chest. Jim talked about Jesus' love, but rather than just saying the words, they were alive inside him. The odor that turned his stomach now became the loveliest fragrance.

Jim felt as if Jesus was saying, *Jim, if you and your wife have any value to me, if you have any purpose in my work—it has to do with this odor. This is the smell of the world I died for.*

Though I've heard and read many stories, I've never forgotten this one. The words, *This is the smell of the world I died for,* have echoed through my mind and spirit on numerous occasions, reshaping my attitudes and responses to situations and people.

These words of God are also lived out at a church that holds a special place in my heart—Scum of the Earth Church in Denver, Colorado. Founded by the band members of Five Iron Frenzy and our friend Mike Sares, the church is designed to reach those on the margins of society. The funky name of the congregation is based on

1 Corinthians 4:12–13: "And we toil, working with our own hands; when we are reviled, we bless; when we are persecuted, we endure; when we are slandered, we try to conciliate; we have become as the scum of the world, the dregs of all things, even until now."

The homeless, the skater punks, the Goths, the multipierced and multitattooed, all find a home at Scum of the Earth. A few years ago, Pastor Mike dubbed anyone who smokes outside the church a greeter, so when you come to Scum, anticipate walking through a cloud of smoke before entering the service.

At a recent Scum evening service, I sat toward the back between an older intoxicated couple and an incoherent homeless man. The couple lacked a filter of any kind—they spoke every thought aloud. Perhaps they thought they were being quiet, but I struggled to focus on the message amidst their steady disruptions. The real distraction was the scent —a blend of pungent body odor, stale beer, urine, feces, and sour breath. I breathed through my mouth to avoid the smell, until I remembered the words God spoke to Jim Cymbala: *This is the smell of the world I died for.*

I quit trying to avoid the smell, and I breathed in Jesus. Born in a feces-filled, urine-soaked stable, the Son of God left the wonders of heaven to enter the muck and mire of our world. The stink filling my nostrils reminded me of the fullness of God's love—a love that goes beyond discomfort and unease to save. This is the smell of love, a scent I want more of in my life.

God can use what he speaks to others to help us recognize his voice and presence in our lives, to stir the hunger to experience more of him. When I hear someone else's story of God providing comfort in their lives, I often find my soul comforted.

Another story that I've never forgotten is of a missionary doctor who faithfully served forty years in the remote villages of Africa. When he decided to retire, he wired a message ahead with the date and time of his arrival. Crossing the sea, he thought of the large homecoming awaiting him in America. Though his heart still beat for the Africans, he knew it was time to return home.

As the ship pulled into port, the missionary's heart leaped with expectation. He scanned the docks. A crowd had gathered, with a huge sign that read, "Welcome Home." This was going to be quite a homecoming. But as the man stepped onto shore, he realized the crowds hadn't gathered for his return but for a movie star aboard the same ship.

He fought to hold back tears as the crowd dispersed. Looking toward heaven, the man half-cried and half-prayed, "God, after giving all those years of my life to my fellow man, was it too much to ask that one person—just one person—be here to welcome me home?"

Within the still quiet of his soul, he heard God whisper, *You're not home yet. When you come home to me, you will be welcomed.*

The story stirs something deep within me. *You're not home yet.* Though I don't use those words, I feel that longing in my heart. The longing reminds me not to become too attached to the pleasures of this world. Even on my best days, when I'm seizing every moment, the hunger in my heart reminds me that this is only temporary housing. God has something far greater in mind, a place where we will be welcomed.

The process of hearing God's voice shapes us. The Scripture compares God to a potter and says we are like clay in God's hands. This rich image describes the transformation that's taking place in all of our lives.

Every potter knows that for a lump of clay to be transformed into a useful object, such as a vase or bowl, the clay needs time on the pottery wheel. After placing the clay on the wheel the potter begins to shape it, using damp hands and steady pressure. Long before the first signs of form or purpose appear, the potter focuses on centering the mass. To the observer, nothing seems to be happening, but this step is crucial. Any imbalance or misalignment in the clay at the start means disaster at the end. Once the piece is shaped and decorated, a glaze adds color and texture to the design before being fired in the kiln. After cooling, the creation is ready for service.

The work of the potter parallels my spiritual hunger to know and serve God. I ask God to

center me,

open me,

balance me,

mold me,

shape me,

trim me,

adorn me,

strengthen me,

perfect me,

and use me.

I long for God to have his way and accomplish his work in me, an impossible task without his hands, reaching into my life.

Shaped through Conviction

Sometimes God uses unusual circumstances in order to reveal our own hearts. In Second Samuel, the prophet Nathan approaches King David with a compelling story.

Two men lived in the city—one rich, the other poor. The rich man had flocks and herds of animals, but the poor man had only a little ewe. The lamb was more than a food source or even a pet. The ewe ate from his plate, drank from his cup, and snuggled against his chest. The lamb became like a daughter to the poor man—a source of comfort and companionship. The wealthy man decided to throw a feast. Rather than take a sheep from his own flock, he took the poor man's only ewe.

When King David, who grew up in the desert caring for flocks, heard the story, he was overcome by anger and declared the man should die and demanded restitution. The poor man should be paid back fourfold for his loss. King David's righteous indignation turned on him when Nathan declared David the guilty man from the story. As the anointed king, David had been given wealth, provision, and wives, yet still chose to have Uriah killed so he could marry Bathsheba.

A simple story was used to expose King David's actions and his heart. In response, David confesses his moral failure, acknowledging his guilt and suffering the consequences. As with the story of David, God uses unlikely situations and stories to stir conviction in our hearts and draw us back to himself. God speaks to me often through conviction, a sense that my attitude or actions are out of alignment with God's.

One particularly rough day for me began as a bad hair day and rolled into a bad-everything day. At the end of a long, grumpy afternoon, I laced up my tennis shoes and headed out the door for a run. I needed to vent, and God was the only available option. I spent most of the two-mile trail around my home expressing an entire grocery list of complaints. The Bible says we're supposed to offer up our concerns to God, so I super-sized my offering, pouring out my heart in a thirty-minute gripe fest. As I rounded the final turn toward the driveway, I emptied my final words and emotions, ending my tirade with a groan that was more of a "So there!" than an "Amen."

Staring at the pebbles on the paved road—which often act like ball bearings beneath my feet—so I didn't tumble, one brisk thought flooded my mind: *It's not about you.*

The words weren't original. I'd heard and read them before, but God was now speaking them at an opportune moment, using them to reshape me as I realized that all of my concerns and complaints centered on one person: me. In my hurt and frustration, I had become self-consumed. Over the next few days, *It's not about you* rolled through my mind and spirit. I felt conviction, the invitation of God's Spirit to change my attitude and behavior. I repented for becoming so self-focused.

That bad day is long gone, but the correction God whispered in my heart often revisits me. *It's not about you.* Those words still serve as a wake-up call when I find myself frustrated or discouraged.

I used to cringe at the thought of conviction, believing that God's correction was a marker of my spiritual failure; but I've begun recognizing it instead as one of God's greatest blessings and a mark of his love. Jesus promised to send the Holy Spirit, who rouses the conscious of right and wrong. A repentant response not only removes the impurities that separate us from God but helps us center our heart with God's heart. The process isn't easy. Discipline always feels more painful than pleasant; but when embraced, conviction promises the peaceful fruit of righteousness.

Conviction is like a tangy fruit God uses to nourish us. When we respond to conviction, spiritual transformation takes place in our lives. Our lives are flavored by the renewed presence of God. Beauty is carved into the core of our character. The conviction *It's not about you* doesn't apply only to my grumpiest days, but to all of them. The words are an invitation to embrace an outward-focused lifestyle, placing others' needs above my own. God longs for our holiness, aches for our freedom, and desires our purity. He wants these things more than we ever will. Like a master potter, God will apply just the right amount of pressure to correct and reprove so that we live centered on him.

Shaped through Spiritual Discovery

Have you ever been reading the Scripture and discovered that a particular verse is illuminated like a soloist on a darkened theater stage? Maybe you stumble on a detail you hadn't noticed before or see a story from a whole new perspective. Your understanding of God and the Scripture is illuminated; a Bible teacher provides background context that sheds light on a familiar parable; a song paints a word picture of worship that you've never grasped before; an artist's image stirs your heart for God; a group of children teach an unforgettable lesson about life. As a follower of Jesus, these moments of spiritual discovery are among my greatest delights.

Whenever I discover more about the divine—whether it's a facet of God's character or an insight into his ways—once again I feel like clay on the potter's wheel whose opening is being formed. These experiences expand my capacity to know God, be filled by God, and be poured out for God. They stir the hunger to know God more.

Sometimes these discoveries are subtle, yet they shift the way we see the world around us. One of my recent discoveries comes from the first chapter of Exodus. The king of Egypt recognizes that the Hebrew people are multiplying, and orders a genocide of all male Jewish newborns. Puah and Shiphrah, two Hebrew midwives, refuse to comply. When the king of Egypt discovers their disobedience, he interrogates them. The midwives explain that Hebrew women are not like Egyptian women; they're vigorous, and give birth before a midwife arrives. When the women are dismissed from the king's presence, they return home to continue their work, and the Hebrews continue to multiply.

As I've studied and reflected on this story, I've been impressed with the midwives' strength and courage. I imagine the duo looking over their shoulders whenever a Hebrew woman gave birth, to see if anyone was coming to take the newborn away. With every birth, they risked their own lives to save innocent children. When they were summoned into the Egyptian court, they likely expected the worst. Yet in a divine moment, they were shown favor. These two women were quiet but effective advocates of the greatest social justice issue of their time. Pivotal in the history of God's people, Puah and Shiphrah changed the future of the nation.

I had read the passage describing these valiant women dozens of times in my life, but recently God used it to open my eyes in a new way. This time, I began studying the meaning of the midwives' names. Puah means "splendid"; Shiphrah is translated as "beauty" or "grace." Their account reminds us that God wants to write a story of splendid beauty and grace in all our lives. Even when our roles are small, God does great things with the faithful. Because of the courage of Puah and Shiphrah, Moses survived and led the Hebrew people out of Egyptian bondage.

By diligently drilling down into God's word, a familiar story came alive for me in a whole new way. These discoveries are like mini spiritual feasts. Sometimes they're for sharing with others; occasionally they're for savoring on my own.

One of my recent spiritual discoveries came through a good idea that went oh-so-wrong. A local bakery had donated donuts for the kids at a nonprofit organization where we were volunteering. I thought it would be great if the kids created handmade thank-you cards for the bakery during their crafts hour. I asked my husband Leif, who was helping the boys build bottle rockets during the crafts hour, about the idea. He liked it, but he needed the full hour to launch the bottle rockets. So I approached Sarah, who was making candy jewelry with the girls. She loved the idea and had plenty of time to tackle both projects. In her enthusiasm, she approached the director of the nonprofit about the idea, who told Leif, despite his protests, that the boys would have to make cards too.

During crafts hour, the girls and boys worked on the cards. But when they found out that the thank-you cards were for donuts, they wanted to know when they were going to get the treats. Sarah and Leif promised the kids donuts after dinner, but the children became obsessed. Donuts. Donuts. Who was bringing the donuts? Where were the donuts now? What kind of donuts? Plain? Sprinkled? Cream-filled? One child even wrote, "When do I get the donuts?" inside his thank-you card. We weren't able to use that one.

In the midst of donut-mania, the eight-year-old children reasoned that if their cards weren't good enough, they wouldn't get any donuts. The boys began adding intricate artwork and details to their cards. Instead of taking a few minutes to draw a donut and write their name, they created masterpieces. Meanwhile, Leif watched the clock. Five minutes passed. Ten minutes. Fifteen. Twenty. After half an hour, Leif convinced the last kid to stop working on his card so they could all launch their bottle rockets. The whole crafts hour had turned into a rushed disaster.

Afterward, I couldn't get the scene of the boys' fixation on donuts out of my mind. A common early morning treat, a sticky ring of dough, became a revelation in my life, emblematic of all the distractions that lead God's children away from our ever-loving Father. I began to wonder, *What are the donuts in my life?* Though the words sounded silly, over the next few days I prayed, *God, what is my donut?*

God began to reveal to me various spiritual detours in my life. Like donuts, distraction comes in a lot of different flavors, including work, amusement, and busyness. When I'm distracted, I spend too much energy on some activities and not enough on others. I'm not fully present, nor as connected with God. Like the children and donuts, I need to be aware of the distractions that enter my life and not allow them to get the best of me.

Spiritual discoveries come in the middle of the most mundane moments—during a quiet time or a crafts hour with kids—but they're always worth paying attention to and learning from.

Shaped through Prayer

Some have said that prayer doesn't change God, but only changes us. Yet on several occasions in the Bible, God makes a concession based on a mere human request. Abraham begs God to spare the city of Sodom and he does, at least for a time. Moses pleads for God not to destroy the Israelites for their idolatry, and God decides not to bring destruction on the people. Centuries later, King Hezekiah's life is extended through repentance and prayer. Though

God is omniscient, immutable, and unchanging, such stories challenge us. What if we really do have God's ear through prayer? What if our heart cries make a difference? What if prayer makes a bigger impact than we realize?

What if?

The mere possibility makes me want to pray all the more and persist in prayer even when I don't understand, even in the silence. For me, the invitation to seek God, know God, and ask anything—well, it's hard to resist.

Prayer is God's invitation to engage in the work he is doing around the world. During his life on earth, Jesus demonstrates the importance of prayer. Pressed on every side with countless demands—including transforming a band of ragamuffin believers into passionate disciples—Jesus emphasizes prayer, climbing mountains and crossing seas in order to get away and pray.

If Jesus makes prayer a priority in *his* life, how much more should we? When asked how to pray, Jesus teaches his disciples that prayer includes worship of God, a desire for his will to be done, and a request for daily provision. One must bring forgiveness as well as a desire to be forgiven, and ask for protection from temptation and evil.

Few activities stir the hunger for God like prayer, which opens our eyes to God and others. Through intercessory prayer, we can advocate for others, asking God to heal, restore, and redeem. When we intercede, we ask for God's mercy, healing, deliverance, and blessing on someone else's behalf, and walk in the confidence that God hears our prayers. In the process, our capacity to love and serve others expands. I love how, through prayer, I find myself with a vested interest in someone else's well-being. After I pray for someone, I'm ripe to show kindness.

Just recently I prayed for a local leader who was going through a difficult time with her organization. These prayers fueled my desire to be a source of encouragement in her life—sending emails, taking her to lunch, and being a friend in a more intentional way. Without prayer, I might have been aware of her problems, but not part of the solution.

Praying for my friends is painless; praying for my enemies brings me to my knees. No matter where I go, I find a new nemesis: a person who stands for everything I stand against. I find myself forced to work with people I don't like or agree with. These individuals are the most challenging when it comes to my personal prayer time. Yet when I obey the command to bless my enemies and pray for good things for those who oppose me, the brittle edges around my heart soften. Such prayers keep me pliable in the potter's hands.

As we pray, God may disclose an insight into a person or situation, and reveal future promises or blessings. We may become aware of another person's weakness, a leader's mismanagement, or a governing body's injustice. Sometimes God reveals these insights because he is asking us to speak up. God is calling us to act with strength and grace, calling us to fearlessly fight abuse and injustice. Other times God is entrusting us with information for another reason. Though God unveils an insight, he may not give us the authority or permission to tell others. We have been entrusted with the information for one reason: God is inviting us to pray.

A friend whose walk with God I've always admired tells the story of a pastor's son in her town who survived a terrible car accident. The child suffered a blow to the head, resulting in permanent brain damage; the two sides of his brain separated during impact.

Before Sheila began processing the information, a small phrase dropped into her spirit: *I hold the keys*. She recognized the Bible reference: "I am the Living One; I was dead, and behold I am alive for ever and ever! And *I hold the keys* of death and Hades." An unexplainable confidence arose in her: the child wasn't going to die. Over the next two weeks, Sheila continued to pray. The words "Wake up, Jerrod. Wake up," rolled off her lips.

Sheila felt compelled to visit the boy in the hospital. Though he was in a secure ward, the family permitted her to see him. She felt led to anoint his head with oil and pray against death. With no noticeable response, Sheila returned home; but Jerrod woke up later that night. After a few weeks, he was released from the hospital and fully recovered. Sheila didn't share with the boy's family what the Lord had spoken to her until after he was healed. She knew her role was to pray with faith for healing.

Intercessory prayer means standing in the gap. Ezekiel 22:30 describes the Lord looking for someone who will "build up the wall and stand before me in the gap on behalf of the land" so he will not have to destroy it. God looks for people to pray and become a part of what he is already doing. When we accept that invitation, we will be shaped in profound ways and feel a craving to know and be used by God.

Shaped through Guidance

God doesn't give us all the details of life. Just as a skilled potter guides the clay on the wheel, so God guides us in order to shape us. Though we don't understand, the master potter has a plan and purpose for every movement.

The Bible is full of faithful leaders who walk into the unknown. God shares long-term plans of blessing with

Abraham, but few specifics on how he is going to make Abraham's offspring more plentiful than the stars in the sky. God promises Moses that the Israelites will go free and enter a territory flowing with milk and honey, but he omits details about the long dusty path to the Promised Land. God tells David that he will one day become king, but never fills him in on the particulars of the years he'll spend serving a crazed King Saul. Throughout the Scriptures God gives the greatest leaders guidance on a need-to-know basis. I realize this, yet still find myself begging God, *Tell me more and tell me now.*

When faced with life's decisions, the hunger for God's voice becomes more acute. My relationship with my husband has been marked by transition. Over the last seven years of our marriage, we've moved multiple times not only within his home state of Alaska, where we met, but also back to my home state of Colorado. Leif switched jobs several times, and our roles at work shift on a regular basis. I wonder if we'll ever settle down.

Our biggest year of transition together was the first. After we married, we house-sat in order to save for a down payment on our first home. We were given a place to stay for the first four months. As the time rolled by, we wondered where to stay next. We prayed. We asked God for favor. We let family and friends know our needs. Another

place opened up. This pattern continued for a full year.
We bounced between homes and apartments and trailers.
The last few days in a place would be upon us when the
cell phone rang or we'd bump into a friend in the market
suggesting a house-sitting opportunity. God answered our
prayers by guiding us to the right people at the right time.

For an entire year, we were given a place to stay, and on
occasion were even paid. Moving was stressful—especially
as newlyweds—but I'm amazed how God orchestrated
a full calendar year's worth of free housing. I'm in awe of
divine guidance and provision.

In my perfect world, God would have handed me a calendar
on our wedding day with a full schedule of where we'd be
living and when. Instead, God used chance conversations
with friends and opportune moments to guide our steps.
Though the year was full of challenges and Leif never
wants to pack another box, God's guidance was perfect.

When I think of the guidance of God, I think about
geography, proximity, and chance encounters. I'm learning
to broaden my definition of the Spirit's guidance. God
doesn't just guide the places where we go or the people we
meet; the Lord is involved in the minuscule details of our
lives.

Recently, a longtime friend of ours, who we don't get to

see enough, sat down with Leif and me and said he had been praying for us. As he prayed, he felt one phrase ring through his spirit: *Excel still more*, words from 1 Thessalonians 4:1–2. Our friend knew of all the work we were already doing, but he challenged us to keep going.

Though our friend meant them as an encouragement, these were the last words I wanted to hear. We had just finished a heavy season of travel and work. I felt drained and exhausted. I needed more than rest; I needed restoration of my entire being—mental, physical, and emotional. "Excel still more." *Doesn't he know my gas tank is past empty?* I wondered. *Is this possibly from God?*

I wanted to dismiss the idea, but it haunted me. When I walked into a kitchen where we were volunteering, a room I'd been in dozens of times, I noticed for the first time that over the doorway were three words: *Excel still more*. I decided to spend some time reflecting on the phrase in the Scriptures.

First Thessalonians 4 offers encouragement to the Church at Thessalonica. The people have grown in depth and breadth. They are acting faithfully, but there's still more. Paul challenges them to excel still more in two specific areas: their walk with God and their love for each other.

The context of the Scripture softened my heart. The

invitation to excel still more wasn't about future work or faster speed, but about growing deeper in God and growing closer together. Even in my exhaustion, I still craved more of God in my life and marriage, and *excel still more* reminded me that God also craved more of a relationship with me. I sensed God's pleasure in the words.

I recognize God's guiding hand in these words of encouragement from a friend and in the act of the unknown person who had hung the Scripture over the kitchen door two years before. The guidance of God is evident throughout the normal rhythm of our lives if we have eyes to see and ears to listen.

Shaped through Love

Of all of the followers of Jesus, John seemed to grab hold of the message of God's love the most. I imagine John weathered by the elements, hunched over in a stone prison cell on the island of Patmos. Whenever someone asked him a religious question, he always brought his answer back to the love of God. John talked about God's love with the passion of a madman, as if no other topic mattered.

God's love ripples through everything John wrote: his gospel as well as his three letters. To write with such passion, John didn't just encounter the love of God; he became saturated. Love dripped off everything he did. The secret to his passion was the intimacy he cultivated with Jesus. John is the beloved disciple who rested in Jesus' bosom at the Last Supper. The imagery of reclining into Jesus' arms is a glimpse into the closeness that develops when we spend sacred time with Christ.

We, too, are designed to overflow with the love of God. As the hunger to spend time with God stirs in our hearts, he reminds us of the depths and wonders of his love, and saturates us in the reality of the sacrifice Jesus made in order to have a relationship with us. God will stir the hunger to know him and love him more.

One of my favorite prayers is *God, how can I love on you today?* As I sit in the silence of those words, sometimes I'll feel compelled to sing or read a passage of Scripture, or I'll be reminded of someone with a need I can meet; but on some of the most meaningful days, God simply says, *Just be with me.* I sit in the silence and enjoy stillness with God. No agenda. No words. No challenge. No correction or instruction. Just being together. In those moments, I'm reminded that the heart of faith is simply being with God. I sense God's love. Some of my best friendships reach a level at which we can sit together without having to say anything and still enjoy each other's presence. The same is true for God, and I long to experience that depth of love in my relationship with Christ.

When the love of God overflows in our lives, we cannot help but pour his love on others. As we experience the love of God, we become more attuned to what God loves and how we can serve those around us.

Last summer Leif and I volunteered at a camp for low-income youth. Each week I witnessed the difference a week of camp made in the lives of underprivileged youth. Many counted their week of horseback riding, BB guns, archery, the ropes course, and the giant swing as the best of their year.

While there, I kept noticing items the camp needed. The couches were worn out, a bathroom was in disrepair, more horses were required. These improvements would make a significant difference for the kids and counselors.

As I prayed, I felt God's love swell in my heart. God saw these needs too. I heard the Lord whisper in my spirit, *You have not because you ask not, and you ask not because you have not.* I recognized the first part of the statement from Scripture, but the second part puzzled me. What didn't I have? What prevented me from asking?

Over the next few days, I asked God to explain. The story that came to mind was the woman with the issue of blood who touched Jesus' cloak and received her healing. Of the hundreds crowding around Jesus that day, many were tormented by health issues, but only one is noted for reaching out to Jesus in faith and taking hold of that healing. She believed. She knew what Jesus was capable of. When she reached out, she experienced the love of God.

In his love, God wanted me to reach out and grab hold of him on behalf of the kids at camp.

God, I want more of you, I prayed. *I want to reach out like the woman and receive that which you alone can provide. I want to experience your love.*

A few days later I shared my experience with some friends. They asked what the camp needed; when I told them, they handed me $300. The expression of their love and generosity almost brought me to tears. The following week, the local newspaper advertised an opportunity for a fundraising partnership with a service organization. I helped write the application letter for the camp director; two weeks later we were selected as the winner and received $4,000. Throughout the summer I frequented stores in the community, asking for donations. The whole process was terrifying, but the love in my heart was greater than any fear of rejection. As I shared with boldness the various needs of the camp, I watched in awe as God moved people toward generosity. In the process, I gained a deeper understanding of God as our source of love and provision.

Though God's words are few, they transform us and usher us into greater service and love. If we will listen for God's voice in our prayers and study, if we wait for God to show up in unexpected moments and search for him in vibrant acts of love, we'll find that God will begin fulfilling our hunger as we draw closer to him. Whether we're reminded, *This is the smell of the world I died for, It's not about you, Excel still more,* or *You ask not because you have not,* we're invited to embrace the transforming work of God in our lives and become more like he designed.

.004 Readiness

I walk into church cold. God is nothing more than a fleeting thought. I take my self-assigned seat in the balcony, slide off my sandals, and wait for the music to begin. Impatient and bored, I flip open the bulletin. The usual suspects appear. Vacation Bible School needs volunteers. Men's prayer at 6 a.m. on Thursday. Women's Bible study at 9 a.m. on Tuesday. *Don't they know women have to work at that time?* Canned food donations needed for the local food bank.

The first chords of music begin to play. I stand and mouth the words to a familiar Chris Tomlin song. My eyes wander to the eggshell-colored ceiling panels overhead. I've counted them before. I count them again. One of the elders stands up to deliver the announcements I've just read in the bulletin. We sing another few songs. My husband drops a check in the gold offering plate. The teaching pastor resumes his series on Exodus; I've always enjoyed the tone of his voice. Thirty-six minutes later, we're dismissed.

I don't feel as if I've gone to church, but to a long meeting. Just a few weeks earlier in this exact place I felt my spirit lifted through worship, my heart made tender through giving, and my mind challenged through thought-provoking teaching. In this same seat, I encountered God's presence in a community of believers. Now I feel a million miles away from God. What makes the difference?

All too often it's me.

Every Sunday is different, but when I prepare my heart and mind before I walk into the service, my spiritual appetite for encountering God increases. Such times of preparation vary. Sometimes they include an early morning hike on which I talk to God and enjoy the stillness of his presence. Listening to a few worshipful songs, reading the Scriptures, or sitting in silence before attending church go a long way toward readying my heart for corporate worship. Such preparation requires intentionality. Do I let the morning hours slip through my fingers, or grasp hold of the precious time?

Readying my heart for God isn't just a Sunday morning practice, but something I need to do every day. When I'm intentional about it, I'm more sensitive to the ways God speaks. Recognizing God's voice means cultivating a seeking heart, a biblical heart, an inquiring heart, a listening heart, and a patient heart.

A Seeking Heart

I played hide-and-seek as a child with my friends. We'd take turns searching for the best possible hiding places

—behind thick shrubs, inside empty boxes, under the kitchen sink. I preferred being the one who hid; all I had to do was find a good spot, sit still, and remain quiet. The one searching had to do the work. When I grew older, I was introduced to a game called sardines, a reverse version of hide-and-seek in which the players who find the hidden person join until the last person discovers everyone hiding in the same spot—all squished up against each other trying not to make any noise.

Though I haven't played hide-and-seek or sardines in years, I find that the elements of the game are still present in my relationship with God. At times, I feel as if I'm playing hide-and-seek with God. Jesus draws near. I sense his presence, the tugging at my heart. Christ found me! Other times, God tucks himself behind a truth, a person, a situation, and I'm the one searching for him. I've seen this process happen in corporate gatherings as well. As in sardines, one person might discover Christ in an unexpected way or place, and over time others discover him and join in too. If we want to hear from God, we need to cultivate a seeking heart, one that expects God to speak at unexpected times.

My friend Valerie went mountain biking for the first time this summer. As she and her friends started up the trailhead, they reminded her of one of the foundational truths of mountain biking: Don't look where you don't want to go. She made the steady climb up the trail, but soon fell behind. As the trail narrowed, she looked at the rugged path, then down the steep rocky hillside beneath her, and promptly tumbled headfirst down the mountainside, into a yucca plant. Upside down on the steep incline, she cried out for help, but her friends were too far ahead to hear. She managed to crawl out from underneath the bike, and when she looked up, she saw a pair of mountain bikers on the trail. They paused to ask if she needed any help. She was okay so she waved them on. One of the bikers offered, "Don't look where you don't want to go."

When I saw Valerie the next day, she showed me the long scrapes left by the yucca plant on her arm and waist. She felt as if God had spoken to her through the words *Don't look where you don't want to go* by reminding her that this foundational truth isn't just true in mountain biking. God invites us to fix our eyes on the Lord. If we want our lives pointed Godward, then our focus must stay on him. God tucks himself into our life experiences and reminds us to look for him in the everyday.

Hunger for God compels us to seek the Lord. At times our desire for God overcomes our physical desires, and the ache for God is palpable. Throughout the Scriptures, God is faithful to reward those who search for him. Written during one of King David's low points, while living on the run in the wilderness, he cries, "O God, you are my God, earnestly I seek you; my soul thirsts for you, my body longs for you, in a dry and weary land where there is no water." Though David hides in the wilderness, he doesn't stay there physically or spiritually. When we seek God with our whole hearts and souls, he promises to reveal himself to us.

God places an intrinsic value on seeking him, but often I find myself distracted by the details of whatever compelled me to pursue God. My attention is drawn to the need for an immediate answer to the challenges I'm facing. It's like solving story problems in math class: Two trains, 100 miles apart, travel toward each other at different speeds. Based on the time the two trains departed, what time do they meet? For extra credit, figure out the mile marker at which they pass each other.

All I really wanted was a train ticket out of the class, but since none was offered, I asked friends to help me with the problem. As a student, I wanted the right answer only to earn a good grade and move on to something else. Years later I realize the lessons were never really about trains, calculations, or math skills as much as about learning how to think.

In the same way, seeking God isn't about the methods, the locations, or the spiritual disciplines, as much as about deepening our relationship with God. The process of seeking God increases our awareness of our dependence on him. We recognize our inability to do things on our own. Our posture changes before God as our heart floods with humility and our will is fortified by a readiness to obey.

Seeking God looks different for every person, but consistency is essential. When I wake up in the morning, I make a beeline for the coffee machine, then nestle in the corner of the forest green couch in our living room. I rest my mug on the end table, next to teetering stacks of books, Bibles, and commentaries by my favorite authors. I'll spend time reading, reflecting, and praying. Our dog, Hershey, snuggles under a fleece blanket beside me. In the stillness of the morning, I lift my thoughts Godward. This is one of the consistent ways in which I pursue God. On the mornings when I press snooze on the alarm or become distracted by the day's demands, Hershey sits on the couch near the stack of books, waiting. Sometimes I think God smiles as he uses my dog to remind me of the importance of seeking and spending time with him on a steady basis.

God speaks to people everywhere—on forest green couches, in office cubicles, behind the wheel during a commute, even on noisy playgrounds. Some people hear God anywhere, and throughout the day; others are more likely to hear God speak at a particular time and place.

As I have a primary place in my home that I set apart for

seeking God, I also try to find a special place in the town where we live. In Alaska, my holy hunting grounds were at the glacier. I'd climb to the edge of the cerulean ice to spend time in prayer and offer the heavier concerns of my heart to God. Since we've moved back to Colorado, I've relocated my spot to Red Rocks Amphitheater, an open-air concert venue that offers natural acoustic perfection. The walls of the amphitheater, made of salmon-colored sandstone ledges, slope as much as 90 degrees. From the top of Red Rocks, visitors can view all of Denver in the distance. I'll spend time there hiking and praying, scenes of the city reminding me of the expanse of God. Nearly 10,000 people will gather on a summer evening at Red Rocks to hear the voices of popular musicians, but I come for only one voice. When I go there, God knows I want to discuss something significant. The act of getting in the car and driving to meet him physically represents the spiritual pursuit and hunger in my heart.

Wherever I'm seeking God, I begin by initiating a conversation with him through prayer. The way I'm wired, I've discovered that it's best for me to begin by letting God know everything in my heart. I'm not afraid to be brutally honest with God; he can take it. As my frustrations and fears, doubts and dislikes drain, I find myself emptied of all the things I'm unable to tell anyone else. Then my heart is prepared to hear from God. I ask him to speak to me, and to give me ears to hear the way he is communicating, eyes to see the way he is moving, and a heart ready to respond in obedience.

After I pour my whole self out before God—my innermost thoughts, dreams, and desires—I sometimes wonder, *Is anyone there?* I don't feel any different. I may feel even less peace than I did when I began praying. That's when I cling to the promise of the psalmist: "The eyes of the Lord are toward the righteous and His ears are open to their cry." I have to remind myself that I'm seeking God because I need him. Any distance or silence I experience is part of being the seeker—my least favorite role in hide-and-seek, but one I'm called to as I hunger for God.

A Biblical Heart

God's voice echoes throughout Scriptures. If I want to know God's voice, I must spend time reading and studying the Bible. Apart from Scripture, I cannot know God's voice as quickly, clearly, or with as much confidence. Hearing from the Lord requires developing a biblical heart, one that is familiar with God's Word. The Scriptures serve as a rudder when I'm listening to God, keeping me balanced, setting me in the right direction, and correcting my course.

As I've already shared, God has revealed himself to me countless times through Scripture. Recently, reading the story of Noah, Genesis 7:11–12 caught my attention: "In the six hundredth year of Noah's life, in the second month, on the seventeenth day of the month, on the same day all the fountains of the great deep burst open, and the floodgates of the sky were opened."

Water covered the land until every mountaintop was submerged. That's a lot of water! The phrase "floodgates of heaven" is unusual, and I searched for other places in the Scripture where the term is used. I found only a handful, but one of them stood out. Malachi 3:10: " 'Bring the whole tithe into the storehouse, so that there may be food in My house, and test Me now in this,' says the Lord of hosts, 'if I will not open for you the windows of heaven and pour out for you a blessing until it overflows.' "

When the floodgates of heaven opened for Noah, water fell for forty days and nights. When God throws open the floodgates of heaven for those who are faithful and generous, how much more blessing pours forth? The connection between these two passages serves as a reminder to remain faithful in giving, to practice generosity. In the moments I'm tempted to hold back or refuse to give, I'll sense the Holy Spirit saying, *Remember the floodgates.*

Spending time in the Scriptures expands the library the Holy Spirit uses to speak. The Spirit selects a story or passage to correct or challenge us. My husband Leif read through several chapters of 1 Samuel when he noticed a subtle but significant shift in the life of Saul. In 1 Samuel 14:35, King Saul builds an altar to God; only a few verses later, however, he builds one to himself (1 Samuel 15:12). As Leif reflected on this rapid transformation, he sensed the question arise in his heart, *Whom are you building altars for?*

The question tapped into deeper issues he'd been wrestling with regarding purpose and worth. He decided to go to his favorite hillside to spend time with God, a place where he builds a rock pile, a physical representation of an altar, to demonstrate his desire to honor God with everything.

Everyone has different methods for reading and studying the Bible. My friends memorize long portions of Scripture and their abilities amaze me. I can't remember what I ate for breakfast. I have a hard time quoting a passage along with chapter and verse so when I do memorize a passage I focus on the chapter number.

Rather than memorize long passages, I've learned to focus my efforts on shorter verses and general placement of stories within the Bible. I'll outline a book of the Bible chapter by chapter, memorizing the placement of the stories and how the themes of Scripture flow together. I can't quote the Prodigal Son parable, but I know it's in Luke 15. If someone asked me about the story of Joseph, I'd calculate that Genesis contains fifty chapters, Joseph makes his first appearance in chapter 37, and his story closes out the book. This discipline has expanded my understanding of the Scriptures and helped me locate passages and phrases when I feel as if the Holy Spirit is bringing them to my mind. I've also found it helpful to hand-copy passages on cards and place them around the house. Some people prefer to hand-copy large portions of Scripture.

For friends who are new to reading the Bible, consider diving into one of the rich portraits of Jesus found within the Gospels. For the creative, artsy personalities, I recommend the gospel of John. For those who prefer brevity, the gospel of Mark is a fine choice. For those who are more scientific in their thinking, the gospel of Luke highlights the miracles of Jesus and should be read with the book of Acts, which is written by the same author and highlights the birth of the church. Find a Bible translation that's easy to understand. Read through one of the Gospels and then begin going through a second time at a slower pace. Reflect on the words Jesus used and the messages delivered. What issues did Jesus choose to address during his short time in ministry? What did Jesus applaud? What disappointed him? How did he interact with people? Look at Jesus' words and life and be open to what he speaks through the Scriptures.

Studying the Bible not only helps us become more familiar

with the stories, cadence, and rhythms of the writing, but with God. Even without hearing a specific whisper from the Lord, we begin to learn what pleases him. Sometimes without even asking, the answer will be there.

An Inquiring Heart

I can ask God any question without hesitation. God invites me to lay myself before him wholly—without reservation—expressing every question and concern. Though he knows my heart's desire before I utter the first word, God welcomes the inquiry as an expression of my hunger for him. He invites me to take the questions of both my head and my heart to him in prayer.

What's the difference between head and heart questions?

I can ask anyone a head question, but heart questions I reserve for dear friends. The nature of a heart question reveals something intimate—quiet fears and reserved doubts. A head question asks, *Why do bad things happen to good people?* A heart question takes the same inquiry but adds a tender pulse: *Why do the storm clouds of life seem to follow my friends no matter where they go or what they do?* People rarely voice such questions in public, and when they do, a kind of hush fills the room, as if something improper has been said.

Growing in my relationship with God, I've discovered the

importance of learning to ask the heart questions and pray with courage. I know God doesn't answer on many issues —but still welcomes the inquiry. Throughout the Bible, God asks tough questions of people just as people ask difficult questions of God. Even Jesus asks his own Father a rather scandalous question: whether someone else could drink his cup of impending death. The answer is no, but Jesus was bold enough to ask. In the book of Job, Satan and God exchange questions, none of which have ready-made Betty Crocker answers.

I'm convinced that everyone has at least one heart question for God. Asking it is one of the things people crave the most in their hunger for him. Some have dozens, even hundreds. Odds are you have one of your own. Pause for a moment:

If you could ask God anything, what would you ask?

Don't pull any punches. What have you wanted to ask for years? Though honest heart questions startle us, I've discovered that God refuses to pull back, turn aside, or duck from such questions. God invites the questions and even asks a few of his own. It's a powerful invitation indeed, because the responses God provides, when he does answer directly, aren't typically the ones we anticipate.

This principle is beautifully illustrated by the encounter of Jesus and his followers with a man born blind. Raised in a culture and religious belief system that taught illness was a result of sin, the followers ask Jesus whose sin caused the illness—the man's or his parents'? They're asking a tough question: Why did this happen? Who is responsible?

Though the Scriptures don't say, I imagine the disciples took an informal poll. Maybe half vote for the man, the other half for his parents. Jesus' vote will break the tie. The disciples wait for his response.

Jesus tears up the ballot. Neither the man nor his parents sinned. The man lived in darkness for years in order to display the vivid work of God in his life. The third option stuns the disciples. They watch in awe as Jesus spits on the ground, places mud on the man's eyes, and instructs him to wash at the Pool of Siloam. The man obeys and returns with 20/20 vision.

The man's wholeness begins with a challenging question: "Rabbi, who sinned, this man or his parents, that he would be born blind?" Jesus does not shrink back, but uses the query to open his followers' eyes and hearts to a whole new way of thinking: some things exist solely for the glory of God. When we seek God and ask the hard questions, God surprises us with answers that shift our understanding of him.

No matter what we're facing, we're invited to inquire of

the Lord, in everyday life and also as we're studying the
Scriptures. I've learned the value of bringing my inquiring
heart to Bible study. I ask God about portions I don't
understand. I'll search for answers in commentaries and
concordances, sometimes without resolve. My Bible is
dotted with question marks alongside verses and stories
that puzzle me or hint at a deeper meaning. For me, the
question marks are a quiet prayer to God that I want to
understand more. Over the years, I've discovered that God
doesn't withdraw from my inquiring heart. We have the
privilege of asking God to give an insight, to reveal things
that are hidden. Ask. And keep asking.

God promises to reveal the depths of the divine to those
who seek him. Daniel 2:22 describes God as one who
"reveals the profound and hidden things; He knows what
is in the darkness, and the light dwells with Him." Christ
reveals God when he tells parables and "utter[s] things
hidden since the foundation of the world" Paul reflects on
this hidden wisdom as "God's wisdom in a mystery, the
hidden wisdom which God predestined before the ages to
our glory." As we seek God, we need to inquire of him.

A Listening Heart

After we inquire of the Lord, we need to take time to listen.
David discovered the power of inquiring and listening at
an early age. Throughout 1 and 2 Samuel, he inquires of

the Lord and waits for an answer. Many of his questions concern upcoming battles. Will the Israelites win? How should they attack? David knew he could never listen to the Lord too much.

A brief but significant moment in David's life is tucked away in 1 Samuel 23, when he is informed that the Philistines are fighting Keilah and looting the land. The news couldn't have come at a worse time. David and a militia of about six hundred men are on the run from King Saul, who is paranoid that the young, popular David is going to seize his throne. With a target on their backs, David and his men move from place to place, staying a half step ahead of the crazed king. The news of Keilah reads like a side note, and David could have dismissed the distress call, knowing he had enough battles to fight already. At the other extreme, he could have charged immediately into battle, convinced he needed to defend everyone attacked by the Philistines. Instead, David inquires of the Lord and waits for his response before making a decision. God instructs him to attack the Philistines and save Keilah.

Like David, we face countless needs and opportunities in life. With each one, we are invited to inquire of God and listen for his response.

Hearing God's voice requires a listening heart. Mastering the art of listening is one of my greatest challenges. As a wordsmith, I've found myself developing a terrible habit: I tend to jump in and finish people's sentences or thoughts. I've been disciplining myself to remain silent. As I'm refining this area in my life, I've wondered how often I do this to God. How often do I cut God off, assuming I already know what is going to be said? Do I try to put words into God's mouth?

The art of listening for God invites me into a realm I find uncomfortable: silence. I must quiet my heart and embrace the stillness that allows me to truly know that he is God. While this may sound counterintuitive, silence is a key to satisfying hunger for God. When you think about feeding your appetite, you might have visions of rushing up to a dining room table filled with savory chicken and side dishes that smell like Thanksgiving. But sometimes rushing the meal is the worst thing we can do. God wants to feed us, and we must learn to sit quietly as he serves a banquet for our souls.

Silence asks me to close my mouth in order to open my heart. The first few moments of silence are the hardest, as I become painfully aware of the hum of the refrigerator, the muffled clang of the dryer. In the stillness, a wave of chores left undone crashes over me. The dishwasher needs emptying. I count seventeen pieces of lint on the carpet. When was the last time I vacuumed? I fight back the distraction with a prayer: *Jesus, help me to focus wholly on you and hear from you.* I say his name a few times. My mind, body, and spirit embrace the silence as a gift. As my listening sharpens, I realize that silence has its own beautiful rhythm. In this place, I'll ask God, "What's on your heart?" and wait.

Sometimes I hear nothing at all, but at others I'll begin thinking of someone long forgotten. Or I'll remember the need of a particular friend. Whether my mind drifts to politics or social justice issues, I offer up prayers to God and pepper him with questions. *Why does this matter to you? What's your perspective? How can I serve you?* At times, I'll feel compelled to pray, serve, or give. Other times, I'll simply sit in the silence with a renewed awareness of what's important to God.

These moments have taught me that God is passionate about the poor, he aches for justice, and he longs for relationship. I've learned about the tenderness of God, discovered new depths of divine love, and treasured the sweet moments of simply being with him.

Listening forces me to learn patience. Nowhere in the Bible does God commit to running on our schedule or fitting into our time frame, though I wish it were that easy! God answers some prayers in the moment, but on others he waits. Abraham and Sarah waited long past their prime to hold the infant Isaac in their arms. Joseph waited years for a family reunion. Martha and Mary had to wait for Jesus to respond to their plea for their brother's healing, and in the meantime Lazarus died. Waiting isn't easy and doesn't always deliver the answer we desire. Learning to hear, recognize, and discern the ways in which God speaks isn't snappy. But in the waiting time, God works within us in ways that are unrecognizable at first but over time reveal their priceless worth.

The art of listening to God doesn't end when the stillness is replaced with the busyness of chores and daily projects; it's only beginning. Throughout the day, I must be sensitive to God's nudges. I need to pray with eyes wide open to see the colorful ways in which God answers, with ears ready to hear the divine orchestrations in my life.

Sometimes after listening for God, I'll find myself questioning what I think I heard. Was that God or my imagination? Was God speaking a divine will or was I trumpeting mine? On occasion, I'll find myself backpedaling—thinking at first that God said yes, now believing it was no. Oh, to develop a listening heart that can handle second-guessing and the cloudiness of confusion!

I've learned to listen while taking a long walk, spending an afternoon with a friend, or running errands. I'll step back to allow my mind and emotions to rest. Then, I revisit the issue through prayer and study, now with a greater sense of clarity. In humility, I ask God to confirm what he's saying.

Confirmation is a wonderful gift from God. Often when God speaks, he doesn't just whisper but echoes — speaking the same truth into our lives in multiple ways. We may sense God speaking something during our time of study, then discover the weekend sermon is on the exact same topic. Later in the week, while enjoying lunch with a friend, the topic comes up again. Toward the end of the week, a friend sends a card with the exact same message! I call those serendipitous moments Sacred Echoes. They allow us to walk more confidently into all that God has for us. Listening to God for all the ways he speaks has taught me that God has more to say than I ever imagined.

A Patient Heart

If patience is a facet of the fruit of the spirit, then most days I feel as if my fruit has been knocked off its tree. Yet learning to blossom and nurture the growth of patience in my life is essential to hearing from God.

God invites us to wait on and with him. In the process, we discover more of his character and presence in our lives. Throughout the Scriptures, men and women wait patiently for God to speak, and Daniel is one of the few who is given a glimpse as to why. Daniel 10:12 – 14:

> Do not be afraid, Daniel, for from the first day that you set your heart on understanding this and on humbling yourself before your God, your words were heard, and I have come in response to your words. But the prince of the kingdom of Persia was withstanding me for twenty-one days; then behold, Michael, one of the chief princes, came to help me, for I had been left there with the kings of Persia. Now I have come to give you an understanding of what will happen to your people in the latter days, for the vision pertains to the days yet future.

The passage hints at the possibility that unseen powers can cause a delay in a response from God. While such explanations stir the imagination and stretch our theology, biblical descriptions of leaders patiently waiting on God are even more intriguing. When Moses went up on Mount Sinai, the glory of the Lord settled on the mountain. According to Exodus 24:16, "the cloud covered it for six days; and on the seventh day He called to Moses from the midst of the cloud." The chronology here seems to reflect back on the timing of the story of creation; but why must Moses wait? Why must any of us wait?

Waiting fills the Old Testament and floods the New. Waiting is carved into history and into the future of God's people. But how will we wait?

Hearing from God invites us to wait patiently as we recognize our posture and place in relation to him. In everyday life, the more we wait to eat, the hungrier we become. Waiting increases our hunger level. With God, waiting is a crucial part of both stirring and satiating our holy hunger. God is all-knowing, yet he chooses to reveal snapshots in his own time. In Acts 20:22, Paul says, "And now, compelled by the Spirit, I am going to Jerusalem, not knowing what will happen to me there."

In the face of silence and uncertainty, Paul's faith blossoms. He doesn't know what's going to happen; he knows only that God will be with him. He writes, "I only know that in every city the Holy Spirit warns me that prison and hardships are facing me. However, I consider my life worth nothing to me, if only I may finish the race and complete the task the Lord Jesus has given me—the task of testifying to the gospel of God's grace."

The Holy Spirit whispers that prison is around the corner, and Paul must wait, not knowing the form or length of imprisonment. With limited knowledge, but focused on God, he doesn't lose heart or hope.

Like Paul, we will face many seasons of the great unknown. We'll find ourselves asking questions, wondering what's next, waiting in the land of in-between. The waiting nurtures patience in our hearts before God, if we allow it. When we learn to wait well—not grasping for what isn't ours or clutching to the past—our faith grows, and our ability to hear from God becomes more fine-tuned.

In the silence, we sometimes discover that God is answering with himself. Remember the story in 1 Kings 19 of Elijah on the mountainside. Elijah pours his heart out to God, and instead of answering, God presents Elijah with himself. This biblical pattern is accentuated when Job questions God, and instead of an explanation God responds with a soliloquy about the divine.

Sometimes the silence of God *is* the message—perhaps a signal for us to pursue God, a reminder of our dependence on God, an invitation to wait. Though it feels uncomfortable and awkward, the silence beckons us to embrace the mystery and marvels of God. Silence can cause us to go to great lengths to get God to say something, anything. But when we embrace God's silence as a different facet of his voice, then we're in a better spiritual posture to recognize what the Lord is saying.

When all *we* hear is silence, sometimes God is trumpeting a message to others. When I read the prophets' and psalmists' stories of crying out in agony, I wonder how they bore the weight and pain of the silence. I'm grateful they did, because their lives paint a rich portrait of faith.

Silence becomes dicey when we're forced to make a

decision. Maybe the lease is up. If we don't move, we'll be fined or even arrested. Maybe the mortgage is due, and the bank won't take no for an answer. Maybe the event is tomorrow, and the last flight there leaves in an hour. We're forced to act one way or the other.

Pinned into a corner by circumstance, we must remember that God is still with us and desires our best. Study and know the promises of God and reflect on any promises or whispers given before the silence. Cling to them knowing that God likes to stretch and strengthen our faith. God often waits until the last hour to move on our behalf. Remain patient and expectant for what God will do.

An Obedient Heart

God is constantly on the move. I cannot stay where I am and follow God at the same time; responding requires movement.

Hearing from God creates a fresh opportunity to respond in obedience. As we grow in obedience, our capacity to recognize God's voice expands. When we close our hearts to him, our capacity to hear God diminishes. In grace, God continues to speak to us even when we are slow to react or refuse to obey, but it's never the same as if we had responded in obedience in the moment.

In trying to sort through what's from God and what's not,

I sometimes find myself paralyzed with doubt and fear. *Am I hearing clearly? What if I'm wrong?* While it's healthy to ask these questions, if I act only when I have 100 percent certainty, I'll never take the first step of responding in obedience. The fear of being wrong prevents me from ever being right and discovering God in a new way!

God knows how to handle my biggest mistakes. When I jump into the deep end of the pool and land with a stinging, awkward flop, God still uses the splash for his glory.

Several years ago, I was at the beach with some Christian friends when I noticed a man sitting nearby. As I watched him, my heart melted with compassion. I felt in my heart that God wanted to bring about some sort of reconciliation between the man and his siblings. I mentioned to one of my friends that we needed to talk to him. Avoiding the "thus-saith-the-Lord" approach, I opted for the safer, "How's it going?" and "What's your name?" The conversation progressed, and I asked him about his family. When he told me he was an only child, my heart dropped. I had belly flopped.

As my friend continued talking with the man, the conversation began taking on a life of its own. Before I knew it, my friend and I had shared the good news of Jesus with this stranger and invited him to church.

Sometimes we aim for a swan dive but end up with a belly flop that God uses to splash cool water on someone's soul. Now, I don't enjoy spiritual belly flops. They sting and they're embarrassing, but I'd rather approach God and say, "I wasn't sure that it was you, but I took the plunge, trusting you for correction if I was wrong" than never step off the diving board.

God loves honing obedience in the simplest of situations. I've lain in bed aching for sleep when a thought popped into my mind: "Your car headlights are on." Now, I have two choices: roll over and try to get some rest, or get up and check. If I get up and the car headlights are on, I know God's Spirit was at work. If I discover the lights are off, no harm done. But if God is trying to get my attention and I stay in bed, then a dead car battery in the morning will be my reminder of a missed opportunity. The more I act on God's promptings, or what I perceive as promptings, the more familiar I become with discerning his voice.

Obedience reflects our love of God. One of my favorite promises in the Bible is based on our willingness to obey. Deuteronomy 28:1–6 says that if we are willing to fully obey the Lord and follow his commands, the blessings others pursue but never lay hold of will follow us wherever we go. Wherever we live, we will find our children, our crops, and our animals blessed. We will experience the delight of God's blessings in every area of our lives. The obedient are promised rich rewards.

How important is obedience? At the end of delivering the Sermon on the Mount, a passionate call to love God and others with abandon, Jesus concludes with the story of two homebuilders, both of whom likely used quality building supplies. One chooses to begin construction on a rock foundation, while the other opts for sand. After the rains fall, only one home still stands. The spiritual lesson is highlighted in the difference between the two foundations: one person listened and obeyed God, building on the rock; the other just listened, constructing his home on sand.

Through obedience, we develop a spiritual muscle I like to call the Knower. New and veteran followers of Jesus strengthen the Knower each time they sense God's Spirit in their lives and respond in obedience. The Knower is an internal track record of experiencing God that allows you to move forward in the confidence that you've heard from him. For example, when you follow the Spirit's leading to call someone, and the conversation ends with that person telling you how much they needed the call, the Knower gains strength. Or when you respond to the holy nudge to give to someone and then discover they had been praying for that exact provision, the Knower becomes stronger.

The Knower grows inside of us when we spend time with

God and obey him. In the process, we become familiar with the ways, the tone, and the presence of the Spirit in our lives. The Knower is a powerful muscle, but not infallible. Even veteran believers can be wrong. But after a while, we develop an ability to hear God's voice, enabling us to courageously respond in obedience.

As we seek to obey God, one of the hardest answers to hear is no. The gospel of Luke tells the story of Jesus' encounter with a rich ruler who asks what he must do to inherit eternal life. The young man's well-polished, well-fed appearance must have stood in stark contrast to Jesus' travel-worn look. Yet Jesus doesn't soften his reply for the young man: "One thing you still lack; sell all that you possess and distribute it to the poor, and you shall have treasure in heaven; and come, follow Me."

In essence, Jesus tells the young man, "No, something else must change in your life." Jesus spoke hard words to the rich ruler and sometimes speaks them to us. We must choose whether or not to obey.

Over the last few years, I've asked the Lord for guidance and wisdom on whether or not to pursue multiple opportunities and heard, "No." Only recently have I seen glimpses of what would have been the result of disobedience. In every situation, I thank God for saving me from heartache and disappointment.

I'm beginning to realize that *no* is one of God's kindest replies. The Lord knows what is best for us, and when we are reaching for bronze, God reminds us that gold is available if we will just wait.

Becoming attuned to God's voice requires intentionality. In the Sundays following the church service that felt so dry, I began setting my alarm clock earlier and taking time to connect with God through prayer and study before I entered the church. To be honest, for the first few weeks, nothing really changed. I still felt disconnected and distracted by ceiling tiles. But then something did begin to feel different—not in the service, but in my heart. I was no longer singing words; I was worshipping, fully present in the midst of a faithful gathering of believers. I found myself hanging on to every word of the sermon, with elements of teaching haunting me for days to come.

When I look back, I can't help but wonder if maybe in the dryness and discomfort of church, when the service felt like nothing more than a business, maybe God was speaking too—beckoning me to pursue him. Maybe he was exposing the distance in my heart toward him. Maybe God can use anything, including silence, to draw our hearts back to him as we learn to seek him, listen, wait, and obey.

.005 The Language of God

Over the last few years, traveling has become an annoying obstacle course. About the time you surge out of your driveway, your momentum is killed by canceled flights, lost baggage, and overbooked hotels. Leif and I have grown used to these disruptions and discovered a secret along the way: how you approach a customer service agent makes all the difference. Speaking gently and graciously often determines whether or not an agent is willing to go the extra mile. Standing close to the customer service desk, though not too close, with a relaxed body posture, places a stressed customer service agent at ease. Even in situations in which the agent is unable to help, the way we approach and carry ourselves communicates volumes.

Time with customer service agents has taught me the importance of nonverbal communication. We use nonverbal cues more than we realize. While our words, along with their tone and volume, are important, we also need to pay attention to body posture, facial expressions, hand gestures, and eye movement. What we see, feel, display, and experience set the tone for what we perceive. If we truly want to understand someone, we need to note verbal, physical, and emotional details.

God uses multiple verbal and nonverbal cues to get our attention and stir the hunger to know him. That's why we need to notice the context and tone in which God speaks, as well as the ways in which he reiterates the same message to us.

Visions, dreams, and providence are often ambiguous. Throughout the Scriptures, God uses a myriad of words, images, experiences, and everyday items to speak to his people. The Lord uses an inside voice when calling Samuel as a young boy, but an outside one for Moses on top of Mount Sinai. Not only does God use prophets and poets to communicate his heart, but he speaks through years of feast and famine. Jesus employs fish and loaves as well as fields and flocks to teach the deeper truths of God.

We shouldn't be surprised when God uses gardening to reveal an insight about the cultivation of faith in our lives, or waiting for a wave on a surfboard to teach patience. God uses children and grandchildren to reveal what it means to grow in dependence on God and remind us of the simplicity of faith. The possibilities are endless.

Scripture

Isn't it reassuring that the God of the universe can whisper a word to you through the Bible as you sip your seven a.m. coffee? I have found the practice of *lectio divina* helps me recognize God's voice in the text. An ancient practice for studying the Scripture, *lectio divina* invites us to read the Bible slowly and attentively so that we can enjoy God's presence through praying the Scriptures. *Lectio divina* asks us to ruminate on the words, tone, and meaning, to meditate and savor God's Word. Like the Virgin Mary, we are to ponder the words in our hearts. Through reading the text slowly, we may discover the still, small voice of God. A word or phrase may catch our attention and interact with us at some of the deepest levels, informing past and future hopes, memories, dreams, and desires. After meditating on God's Word, *lectio divina* calls us to engage in a loving conversation with God through prayer. The final phase is enjoying his presence in silence through contemplation and resting in him.

I recently used *lectio divina* to meditate on a story from the gospel of Luke. Traveling between Samaria and Galilee, Jesus encounters ten men with leprosy; knowing their affliction is contagious, they choose to obey the law and stay out of the city and away from other people. The men shout to Jesus from a safe distance, asking for mercy. Jesus instructs them to go and show themselves to the priests. They trust Jesus and obey. As they set out for the priests —the only ones with the religious clout to declare leprosy healed and clean (Leviticus 13)—the leprosy disappears. All are healed!

Only one returns to Jesus. Praising God in a loud voice, he crosses every religious and cultural barrier with boldness, flinging himself on the ground to express thanks to Jesus. The writer of Luke goes out of his way to mention the man is a Samaritan—a second-class population in Israel that often suffered discrimination. Yet of this man Jesus asks, "Were there not ten cleansed? But the nine—where are they? Was no one found who returned to give glory to God, except this foreigner?"

As I sit in silence reading and reflecting on this passage, my attention is drawn to the Samaritan. While the others follow Jesus' instructions, this man breaks the social and religious rules that forbid a person with leprosy to touch anyone and throws himself at Jesus' feet. He leaves the pack, disobeying orders, yet Jesus applauds him. Why? The Samaritan is overflowing with gratitude. Were the others thankful? Of course! But only the Samaritan can't contain his thankfulness.

In the silence cultivated through *lectio divina*, one question rolls through my mind: "Where are the other nine?" I commit the words to memory and allow them, along with this story, to interact with my own life. Vivid memories of being disappointed by people's lack of thankfulness flood my mind. The images are so fresh I feel a sharp sting. In thoughtful prayer, I sense God saying, *If only one of the ten turned back to thank Jesus, how can you expect more?* My heart is pierced by this truth.

I enter into a conversation with God, asking for the grace to forgive those who weren't grateful, as well as grace from those to whom I have not shown gratitude. I find myself challenged by the Scriptures and prayer to be more like the Samaritan, overflowing with so much gratitude that I'm willing to break cultural expectations and religious rules to show it. As I pray, the echoing phrase in my mind is *Be the one!* Be the one who sends the thank-you card, who writes the email of gratitude, who goes out of the way to say thank you. Be the one who breaks through shallow conversation to connect on a heart level with others. Be the one who speaks out on issues no one wants to discuss. Be the one who isn't afraid to look silly in gratitude to God. Be the one who turns back when everyone else has left. Be the one!

Sitting in the peaceful presence of God, I find myself grateful for his voice in my life, and enjoy these stolen moments with him. Studying the Scriptures using facets of *lectio divina* expands my capacity to hear from God and awakens me to biblical truths I'd otherwise overlook.

Liturgy

As a child, I found the liturgy at formal church services dry and rote. But as I've grown older, I've found myself falling head over heels for the Book of Common Prayer and selected Scripture readings.

My appreciation of liturgy compounded as I recognized the layers of depth, beauty, and symbolism as potent reminders of the character of God and his faithfulness. Liturgy means "the work of the people" and serves as a reminder that we all have an active role to play in bringing glory to God.

On a recent Sunday morning, Leif and I attended a tiny mountain town church. Above the organ pipes, a large wooden cross draped in purple cloth represented the royalty of Christ. As the service progressed, we offered our praise, confession, silence, and prayers. We lifted our hands as a congregation to bless the children and listened as the words of a timeless hymn swept over our souls. After a passionate call to follow Christ at all costs, the pastor tore a loaf of bread in half before our eyes, then lifted a goblet and pitcher that had been formed by a local potter's hands. The sanctuary filled with the sound of the pouring of the sacred liquid, which ended with a slight clank as the goblet and pitcher collided. I felt as if I had witnessed a miracle, the miracle of the Eucharist.

The attention to detail throughout the service awoke my senses to God. The sounds, the tastes, the smells, and the sights remind me that God is in the details, calling out if only I will wait, watch, and listen.

I love liturgical churches. Scripture readings are central and the beauty of the Bible glimmers at every turn. Each act and expression has value, every word of the brief sermon carries weight. Some of the most incredible Sunday morning teachings I've ever heard were at liturgical churches where the sermon lasted less than twelve minutes.

Liturgy reminds me that faith isn't about adapting to the world's whims, but about discerning and obeying God's calling on our lives. Within the liturgy, everyone has the opportunity to announce their faith, confess their sins, and worship God in unity. God speaks through liturgy and often uses the signs and symbols of liturgical elements to breathe life and hope into us.

God has spoken to me through liturgy by way of its steady practice. Liturgy asks me to calm my spiritual restlessness and center my mind, will, and emotions on Christ. The discipline of engaging in liturgy invites me to enter the enduring story of faith that has been passed down for generations, and reminds me that following Jesus is meant to be lived out in community.

Liturgy provides a context in which God often speaks to us. Last Sunday, one of our liturgical readings focused on Proverbs 19:1–2: "Better is a poor man who walks in his integrity than he who is perverse in speech and is a fool. Also it is not good for a person to be without knowledge, and he who hurries his footsteps errs." After the reading, we entered a time of confession, and I was reminded of a friend whose slow response to making decisions at his workplace had become bothersome to everyone who worked with him—including me. Yet as I meditated on the verse, I realized my friend was only trying to be strategic. I confessed my impatience, and over the upcoming week my attitude toward him softened.

Not only does liturgy illuminate God; it also directs our hearts toward God, inviting us to be the people we're created to be. Liturgy reminds us that God speaks through routines and the mundane, often when we least expect it.

God Thoughts

Throughout the Bible, stories abound of God speaking in an audible voice. I've known followers of Jesus who have experienced the externally audible voice of God, but I never have. God has spoken to me only through internal impressions or phrases that come into my mind, and I believe that most people are likely to hear the voice of God in this way.

The Holy Spirit is described as both a counselor and the Spirit of truth. Jesus promises that as followers, the Holy Spirit will come and take up residence within us. We can expect the Spirit to counsel us as we pray. The internal audible voice is like an external one, except that you don't hear it with your ears, but with your spirit. I call these God Thoughts—those impressions, phrases, or ideas that resonate within your being and come from above.

With God Thoughts, you know the impression or feeling originates with God. You pray about your future, then suddenly find yourself praying for a family member. You think about your job only to feel overwhelmed with compassion for a coworker in need. You listen to the Lord and sense God's overwhelming love and compassion pour over you. These out-of-the-blue thoughts and impressions are often from the Father.

The clarity and boldness of God Thoughts sometimes makes me wonder if God really did speak aloud. While praying about a particular issue, a single word may echo in my spirit. I've prayed over issues and sensed the words *no, go, wait,* or *not now.* As I prayed, I felt like one of those words was alive inside of me, taking root and refusing to budge. Through prayer, I'll wrestle with God through questions like, *God, if this is really you, please show me in Scripture,* and *God, if this is really you, I'll need you to confirm this,* then watch expectantly for the ways he responds.

Over the years I've wrestled with many insecurities, but something about speaking in public brings all of them to the surface at once. Some people deal with stage fright better than others. I'm a low-scorer. Before I address an audience, my mind is flooded with self-destructive thoughts. My gawky, klutzy, acne-marked teenage self reappears in the span of about three minutes or less. And I still have another half hour before it's time to present.

My mind wanders to speakers who are far more gifted communicators. I second-guess the hosts who invited me. As the time draws closer, my stomach knots. I dash to the restroom for relief, then rush back to the stage to wait out the torturous last moments. Three. Two. One. Go.

When will it stop?

After dozens of rounds of this anguish, I decided to ask God about my self-doubts and insecurities. Where did they come from? What needed to change? I prayed and searched the Scriptures for months without reply. With a busy travel schedule, I learned to endure the tormenting stage fright.

After months of silence from God, I reached a place of

honesty in prayer. The flood of dark thoughts was rooted in my insecurities and lack of self-worth, but instead of trying to hide them from God, I took them to him. I prayed, "God, You have created so many people who are *more* in every sense of the word—more intelligent, more spiritual, more knowledgeable, more eloquent, more attractive, more everything—why do you ask me to do this when so many others do it so much better?"

As I prayed, a God Thought penetrated my mind: *All I desire is for you to be you and for you to be mine.*

That's it, I thought. *That's all God's asking.* The stress I experienced was of my own creation. God wasn't asking me to be anything more than he made me to be. In that moment, I laid hold of a new sense of freedom. The next time I stood backstage, when the familiar tidal wave of self-doubts crashed over me, as if on cue I remembered the God Thought: *All I desire is for you to be you and for you to be mine.*

Oh. I can do that. The dark thoughts stopped. Each time another wave broke over me, I'd say aloud, *All I desire is for you to be you and for you to be mine,* and I'd find myself once again centered into the reality of God's presence in my life.

During the following months, I found myself more comfortable in my skin than I'd ever been before. I also stumbled on a rich observation by poet e.e. cummings: "To be nobody-but-yourself in a world which is doing its best, night and day, to make you everybody else—means to fight the hardest battle which any human being can fight; and never stop fighting." No matter what situation I find myself in, the invitation of God remains the same: *You be you and you be mine.*

Visions

Visions take different forms for different people. Some people see open-eye visions: looking at one thing in the natural realm, they see something different in the spiritual one. Other people receive closed-eye visions and describe seeing in their mind's eye. Let me give you an example: Close your eyes for a moment and picture a tree with a thick, round trunk and emerald leaves. Can you "see" the sturdy, vibrant tree in your mind's eye? Likewise, people who have closed-eye visions can see what God is showing them.

Ezekiel, Daniel, Luke, Acts, and Revelation are only a few of the books of the Bible in which followers of God receive visions. Isaiah has a remarkable vision of God sitting on the throne with his glory filling the temple, Nebuchadnezzar has a vision about his future, and Paul sees Ananias praying for him to receive his sight before it happens.

Visions aren't common for me. I've only experienced a handful, but fifteen years ago one vision impacted my understanding of God.

On a mission trip to Honduras, we visited a small church during its Sunday morning service. I sat in the front row wearing a loose cotton blouse and oversized skirt—a frumpy missionary fashionista. Though I didn't understand the lyrics, I clapped along with the music and sensed God's presence among the few dozen scattered throughout the congregation.

As I stood with my eyes closed, worshiping God, I watched creation unfold in a series of images. Like a baseball thrown in the air, a ball of light penetrated the darkness and exploded like fireworks. Stars filled the universe. As I watched, one star grew closer until the color shifted to blue. I recognized our planet. Approaching the surface, a cobalt glassy expanse reached in all directions, and small ripples revealed the ocean. The images moved and land appeared on the horizon—at first uniform but then bursting forth with mountains, valleys, deserts, and canyons. Vegetation began sprouting. As the images passed through my mind, I sensed joy and delight and wondered if God had felt the same when creating the heavens and the earth. In the final scene, I saw an image of Jesus, his hands extended, standing beneath a waterfall. Animals of all different

species, birds, deer, monkeys—everything imaginable—
emerged from his hands and filled the earth.

When the final scene of Jesus ended, the vivid images and
presence of God left me shaking. I sat in my chair trying
to compose myself, but every time I closed my eyes I was
reminded of the power and sovereignty of God. The Lord
is truly the beginning, the source of everything. Nothing
comes into being apart from him. I was speechless, in awe
of God.

In the days following the vision, I had an unusual
experience. Every time I looked at something from nature,
I heard, "Glory, Glory, Glory!" Though the voice was
inaudible, the words were loud, even deafening. I closed my
eyes to make them stop. Driving through the mountains
outside of Tegucigalpa, whenever I looked at a peak in the
distance, a tree in the forest, a cow in the pasture, or a cloud
in the sky, I heard "Glory, Glory, Glory!"

I felt as if all of creation was crying glory to God, and for a
short time I was given ears to hear it. Portions of nature I'd
never considered—mud puddles, gravel, brown grass—
cried "Glory to God" with equal fervency. I was reminded
that we're all invited to join creation in the chorus of "Glory,
Glory, Glory" with our lives.

After three days, the cry of creation within my spirit

faded. I still recognized that all of nature glorified God, but the sound was no longer deafening. As I searched the Scriptures over the following weeks, portions of the Bible came alive in a new way, including the story of creation and the words of the creatures around the throne in Revelation.

One passage that I've never read the same since is in the gospel of Luke. Jesus enters Jerusalem and nears the Mount of Olives. A crowd of followers begins to praise God and shout, "Blessed is the king who comes in the name of the Lord! Peace in heaven and glory in the highest!" The Pharisees challenge Jesus to rebuke his followers, but Jesus explains that if the people keep quiet, even the stones will cry out. After my experience, I wonder if Jesus meant what he said: the rocks of the earth will cry out with praise. Maybe they already are, but we can't hear them.

Though the vision took place many years ago, sometimes, when I'm out hiking, I'll hear the faint "Glory, Glory, Glory" in my spirit, a reminder of God's presence throughout the earth and an invitation to join all of creation in praising him.

Dreams

Dreams truly are windows into the soul. They provide guidance, direction, comfort, correction, healing, or insight.

I've met many people who believe God has spoken to them through a dream. For many, dreams from God are rare and may happen only a few times over the course of their lives. For others, they are much more common.

Often difficult to interpret, dreams can require years of waiting to be understood. One of the most famous dreamers of the Bible is Joseph, who dreams he will be greater than his brothers. In a moment of foolishness, he shares the dreams with them. Joseph then spends decades surviving multiple trials—slavery, seduction, imprisonment, neglect—before the dreams come true. Though Joseph undoubtedly questioned the validity of his dreams during his sufferings, God keeps his promise.

God often uses symbols and colors to speak through dreams. I've found it helpful to ask the Lord to reveal what each segment of the dream means. Several years ago, I dreamt about one of my neighbors. I saw a golden light fill her home and explode until everything was dazzling and radiant. I awoke, turned on the light, recorded the dream, and began asking the Lord about it.

In my heart, I knew the gold light represented a blessing from God. I felt that God was going to bless my neighbor, but was puzzled as to why the woman herself had not appeared in the dream. I asked God about it, and remembered that the gold light had exploded in the home, not on an individual person. A thought flashed through my mind: *I am going to bless her household for it is my good pleasure to bless those who are upright and diligently seek me.*

The next morning I awoke early and prayed as to whether or not to tell my neighbor. Around 9 a.m. I felt peace about sharing the dream. Though I knew her well, I felt nervous and stumbled over my words.

When I finished sharing, she said, "When you knocked, I had just hung up the phone with my sister. My brother is developmentally disabled, and it has been a real financial strain on all of us. He just received a letter from the Social Security department saying they miscalculated his benefits, and they're sending him a check for $20,000."

Not only did God answer her prayers, but in his grace I was included in the story of what the Lord was doing and confirmed the dream really was divine.

Throughout the course of your life you will have countless dreams. In some of them, God is speaking; in others, God may not be saying anything. How do you know the difference?

If you are not sure of a dream's source, ask God through prayer to reveal it to you. Ask if he was trying to communicate something to you, and if so, what? Record your dream in a journal and wait patiently for God to reveal the meaning. Consider sharing with someone who also hears from God through dreams.

My friend Naomi recently texted to say she'd had a dream about me and wanted to check in and see how I was doing. I told her that I was struggling but still hanging on. On a whim, I asked her about the dream. She dismissed my interest, saying it was only a result of her own restlessness. I asked her to write down the dream and send it to me anyway. When I read it, I almost wept.

In her dream, she was with a group of happy, vibrant friends that included me. She remembered looking at the faces and thinking, *This is a great group—I'm glad to be in a community of people making a joyful imprint for eternity.* Everyone was engaging in lighthearted laughter, but Naomi could see that even though I, full of spunk and chutzpah, was a ringleader of the fun, I was secretly in pain, living under the shadow of an uncertain and ominous cancer diagnosis. She sensed that a painful inner story ran parallel to the story I was writing on others' lives.

I held back the tears. Naomi's words cut to the core of what I was feeling and brought great comfort. I had recently had a cancer scare, and still wrestled with a mysterious new illness that left me feeling weak and uncomfortable. The night of her dream, I had helped host a party for thirty friends. I enjoyed our celebration, but was constantly

aware of my physical limitations and challenges. Just as
Naomi described, two stories ran parallel in my life—one
of serving and one of struggle. God saw them both and
made himself real in the midst of the situation through the
dream, reminding me that he was still with me. I'm grateful
that God still uses dreams to speak.

Journaling

It's no secret that Leif and I have struggled over the years to
connect spiritually through our personal times of devotion.
In the early days of our marriage, we tried a laundry list of
things that simply didn't work. We began reading Oswald
Chambers together on the first of January one year. By
January 18, we couldn't even find the book. We attempted
reading the same passages of Scripture for discussion, but
also felt a sense of disconnect. We tried reading the same
books and listening to the same sermons, but it always felt
forced, unnatural, and anything but, well, organic. Images
of spiritual marital bliss faded into the reality that growing
spiritually together as a couple takes time, perseverance,
and hard work.

Over the last few years, we've found something that works
—and when we find something that works, we do it and
keep on doing it! We sit on the couch beside each other in
the morning and read different books together. Lately, I've
been loving Bruce K. Waltke's commentary on Genesis; Leif

has been making his way through *The Rest of God* by Mark Buchanan. As we read, we sometimes hmmm or oooh-ahhhh aloud, signifying we've found something special; then we share what we've read and how we responded to it. It's natural. Nonforced. The practice works for us. When we're done, we each read a prayer aloud from Walter Brueggemann's *Awed to Heaven, Rooted in Earth*. Then we spend time praying together.

Brueggemann's writing has been a gift to us. He has the ability to bring the hidden thoughts of the soul to light. Yet his collection of prayers wasn't something that he sat down and decided to write. The prayers emerged during his more than forty years teaching. Each class that Brueggemann taught began with a handcrafted evocative prayer for the day, which is both beautiful and challenging. The prayers' tone echoes the prophets of old and the heart cries of the psalmists. The collection becomes a spiritual journal marking the highs, lows, and self-doubts not only of Bruegermann but often ourselves as we see our own hearts revealed in his words.

Like Bruegermann, those who write their thoughts and prayers often find their hearts exposed. Journaling is a rich spiritual discipline used to communicate with God. Through writing, we lay our fears, frustrations, hopes, and dreams before God in prayer, and create a place to confess sins and find comfort. Journals become sacred places when blank pages are transformed into precious records of reflection and confession. We can slip off the mask of who we are supposed to be and slip into something more comfortable: who we really are.

My friend Bill once shared a powerful story I've never forgotten, about a man climbing a narrow ledge on the side of a mountain. As he approached the top, the trail grew narrower, until he had to walk sideways to avoid tumbling down the mountainside. He pressed his body against the cool stone and took a deep breath.

Then he heard an unexpected voice. "Who goes there?"

The mountain climber tried to identify himself as a friend, not a foe, inching forward to catch a glimpse of the stranger. Beyond a jagged bend in the rock, he saw a thin figure squatting in front of a cave. On the ground beside him rested a goatskin bag.

The mountain climber began a conversation with the hermit about his life on the mountain. When he asked what was in the bag, the hermit explained that he liked to sing; when he felt things deep down inside, he wrote them down. The goatskin bag contained his writings. On a whim, the climber asked if he could read them. Squatting on the thin ledge, flipping through each page, the mountain climber found that he recognized these words. He was reading the Psalms. He realized he'd been given a rare opportunity to see the emotional place from which the Psalms were written.

I'm haunted by this story, which illustrates the dark and difficult places our prayers and songs to God often come from. The Psalms capture the heights and depths of everyday life; they both herald the wonders of God and wave a clenched fist at his silence. The range of emotions within the Psalms is breathtaking, and the most potent are written along the treacherous and lonely ledges of life.

Like the hermit on the mountainside, we have the opportunity to write what we're seeing, feeling, and experiencing in our relationship with God. With pen in hand, we cry out to God, release our inner groans, and celebrate our encounters with him.

Journaling aids other spiritual disciplines. Writing down insights helps Bible study. Writing prayers helps us focus on God. Writing a poem that praises God fosters worship. For many of my friends, God speaks through their journals. Reading old entries serves as a reminder that God heard and answered prayers. Some friends place quotes around the words they feel God is speaking to them. Through the pages of a journal, they hear from God and record rich testimonies of his faithfulness.

My friend Audrey's parents were absent during much of her childhood. As she prayed, she felt that for all the parenting she lacked, God could be a mother and father to her. But while it was easy to wrap her mind around God being a father, she wondered how he would fulfill the role of a mother. She opened her preprinted journal with special quotes on the top of each page, and read the words of Isaiah 66:13: "As one whom his mother comforts, so I will comfort you." With that passage, she felt like God was reminding her that he was both her father and mother promising to always be with her.

Audrey's story reminds me that as our pen meets paper, God's Spirit moves in unexpected ways that satisfy our hunger for God in everyday life.

Conscience

Last year Leif and I were working with a nonprofit organization that needed new computers. We ordered several new PCs, but when they arrived, one was damaged, so Leif returned it for a full refund.

Months later another computer arrived on our doorstep. By this time, neither of us remembered the details of the original order. We double-checked with the nonprofit, and they had received all the computers they were promised. Now we had a mysterious extra computer. I was thrilled!

We didn't need a computer, but I knew nonprofits who were in dire need and looked forward to passing the machine on to one of them.

Leif stifled my excitement when he said we needed to check with the company to find out if they'd made a mistake. I argued that maybe we'd never received the refund. He challenged me to look at our credit card receipts. Drats. They'd sent it months ago. I prayed that when he checked with the company, they'd let us keep it; but they asked us to send it back. Double drats.

I'm embarrassed that I actually became angry with Leif during this time, because more than anything I wanted to give the computer away. Leif's conscience reminded me that my good intentions had another name: stealing.

Though sometimes our conscience feels like an enemy, we need to make it our best friend. God uses our consciences to speak to us and cultivate the fruit of the spirit in our lives. Our consciences challenge the way we manage people, handle our finances, and respond to sticky situations. Everyone has a conscience—an inward sense or feeling that helps us discern between good and evil. Our conscience can direct and guide, but our refusal to respond makes it more difficult for God to speak to us.

Have you ever seen a Western film in which a metal

triangle was used to call people to dinner? A metal rod
inserted in the triangle and rolled around the edges creates
a loud clanking sound. Conscience is like that triangle.
Each time I say or do something that goes against God's
commands, I'm alerted by a feeling of uneasiness, ickiness,
or guilt. When I respond by repenting and doing what it
takes to make things right, my conscience becomes quiet
and clear again. A peaceful calm returns. But if I ignore my
conscience, the clanging sound will grow dimmer. Repeated
sin and refusal to change softens the metal that swallows or
deadens the sound. Conscience can wither.

In all honesty, I knew all along that I needed to check with
the computer company to see if a mistake had been made
in the shipment. But I justified my wrongful attitude and
actions by telling myself that we were going to do good
with the computer. Not only did I apologize to Leif, but I
also let him know how grateful I am for him and the Holy
Spirit's promptings.

Leif reminded me how much all of us as followers of God
need to spur each other on to good and holy behavior.
Sometimes spurring on is messy! In 1 Corinthians 8:1–13,
the apostle Paul addresses a group of believers who are split
over whether or not to eat meat that has been sacrificed to
idols before being sold in the market. Some Corinthians
note that the food is acceptable; but others feel the meat is

wrong to consume on principle, since it has been offered to false gods. Like many of the hot-button issues of today, Paul was addressing a moral question that was grey rather than black or white. Paul responds that love trumps. If eating the meat causes someone to stumble in their faith, then it's better to abstain; otherwise it is permissible. In other words, sometimes love asks us to limit our freedom on behalf of someone else.

Our consciences challenge us to be honest with ourselves and place other's needs above our own. When we pay attention to our conscience and choose to love, we find ourselves living in right relationship with God and one another. Conscience doesn't just remind us of what we *shouldn't* do, but what we *should*, and helps us to see what to do to make things right. Responding to God when he speaks through your conscience will help you go the extra mile to serve, love, communicate, and create vibrant relationships.

Circumstance

God speaks through circumstance as unexpected opportunities ambush our lives. The sudden arrival of an acceptance letter, invitation, or contract can take us by surprise. God may be leading us through the opportunities before us, but he also leads when opportunities disappear. Sometimes doors slam. A job goes to someone else. A

marriage proposal is shunned. Support funds fail to
materialize. A "Sold" sign appears. God can teach us just as
much through a closed door as an open one.

Paul, who we read about in the book of Acts, takes multiple
missionary treks with many legs that seem slow and
unfruitful. On his first trip, Paul travels with Barnabas from
their church in Antioch. They set sail to Cyprus and then on
to Turkey, telling people, mainly Jews, about Jesus. While
many believe the message, others reject it and run them out
of town. On a second trek, Paul's plans are turned upside
down after a fallout with Barnabas, so he settles on Silas
as a travel companion. Then, instead of traveling to Asia as
planned, God redirects his steps to Macedonia, the site of
present-day Greece. They successfully launch the church in
Europe, but not without being thrown into jail. A third trek
to Turkey and Greece is marked by Paul's performance of
extraordinary miracles, but also a riotous response. Toward
the end of his life, Paul is shipwrecked on his way to Rome,
but uses even this as an opportunity to introduce people to
the goodness of God and the story of Jesus.

Paul's travels are never about getting from point A to
point B in a straight line. God uses multiple circumstances
to lead, guide, redirect, and shape the apostle's path.
Throughout the book of Acts, Paul appears all over the map
—literally—in his travels and detours, but God uses these
circumstances to accomplish the divine will.

God can use circumstances to move us in new directions and ambush our best plans. My friend Mark Batterson experienced this firsthand when he felt led to plant a new church in Washington, D.C. During the weekend of the church's first meeting, in January 1996, the city was struck by a record snowstorm. The only attendees at the inaugural service were Mark's wife and son. Despite the circumstances, Mark refused to give up. The following Sunday nineteen people gathered. A core group of twenty-five people continued to meet at a school for the next nine months, until Mark received discouraging news: the school was being closed immediately due to fire code violations.

On the verge of being a church without a place to worship, Mark and his community prayed. High rent and exorbitant property costs forced the church planters to think creatively. They approached the movie theater in Union Station about using the facilities on Sunday mornings, and the theater agreed. Since then, National Community Church has grown and launched multiple locations in movie theaters throughout the nation's capital. God used the challenging circumstance to expand the vision of the gathering and the founders' ability to serve the unchurched.

Circumstance is one of the most challenging ways to recognize God's voice, because it's often unclear where God is leading us. We can easily misinterpret circumstance by jumping to the conclusion that we've been wronged or shortchanged. If only the leadership had been more experienced or had more information, if only I'd tried harder or communicated better, worked smarter or faster, things would have turned out differently. Left to the waves of circumstance, it's too easy to be tossed to and fro among hundreds of possibilities, options, and interpretations.

When you believe God is speaking to you through circumstance, ask him to confirm it through the Scriptures, wise counsel, and a sense of peace.

Counsel and Others

When it comes to learning life's lessons, I try to bypass painful mistakes by listening to those who are older, wiser, and more experienced than I am. Whenever I look for counsel on an issue—whether it's from a spiritual leader, parent, or friend—I seek out people who are grounded in their faith and rooting for me. I want the person I'm talking with to be committed to seeing me grow into all that God has for me; I'm not looking for an opinion as much as for godly wisdom. I need to know the person will pray for me, encourage me, and challenge me at opportune moments.

Throughout the Bible, older Christian men and women pour their energies into aiding younger ones. Elijah mentors Elisha, Naomi offers wisdom to Ruth, and Paul invests in

Timothy. Seeking counsel signals wisdom, not weakness. While we may stumble on to a source of godly wisdom in a pinch, I've found it's best to begin developing those relationships long before a decision-making moment arises.

A decade ago, I received the news that my uncle had died in a scuba diving accident. The news turned my aunt's world upside down. She needed extra help at her bed and breakfast, and so I traveled to Sitka, Alaska, to help her during the summers. On my second visit, I met Leif, a 6'8" guy who I seemed to run into wherever I went in town. We became friends and began dating. After knowing him a month, I was about to leave when he sat me down and asked me to move to Alaska, with the intention of pursuing a relationship to become his wife.

I knew my answer: No way! Who moves to Alaska for a boy? I'd known women who had moved across the country for guys, and their stories never ended well. I packed up and headed back to my home state of Colorado.

Leif continued pursuing me with phone calls, gifts, and notes. We kept in touch, and two months later he traveled to Seattle to meet my mom and me before my cousin's wedding. After spending only a few hours with Leif, my mom pulled me aside and said, "This guy is amazing, and you're a fool if you don't give this relationship a chance." In that moment, my mom was the source of wise counsel and wisdom, speaking words I didn't know I needed to hear. My mom was for me, she loved God, and she was praying that God would provide me with an amazing spouse. I listened to her and moved to Alaska. Less than a year later, Leif and I were married. Without Mom's godly counsel, I may have missed one of the greatest gifts God has ever given me.

Look for opportunities to build relationships with those who are older and wiser in the faith, people you can turn to for prayer and wisdom. Be intentional as well about building relationships with younger people you might be able to help.

Books, Music, Movies, and Other Media

The Hebrew Scriptures radiate the creativity of God and celebrate the richness of the arts. The tabernacle and temple were extravagant in their design. Psalms, Proverbs, Ecclesiastes, and Job are ripe with poetry and pointed prose. Meanwhile, melody and movement fill the story of God. After the Israelites cross the Red Sea, they break out in dancing and singing in their elation. King David is renowned for his godly groove. Even Jesus is a craftsman, a carpenter by trade, and the Bible itself is a wondrous work of art that has inspired countless other works.

I'm grateful God speaks through the arts, and not just because I'm an artist! God uses books and bluegrass, movies and melodies, sculptures and creative expressions to reveal himself and his work in our world. He uses many forms of media—from billboards to bookmarks—to draw our hearts back to him.

Whenever I visit art galleries, my eyes are drawn to the contrasts of light and darkness, and my imagination swirls with the tensions found within. Whimsical expressions and sunbursts of color remind me of the goodness of God. Listening to a Coldplay album, I find myself stirred by themes of searching, transformation, humility, and refuge.

Because I spend so much time writing and reading for work, I prefer other artistic expressions in my free time, particularly television shows and movies. I relish watching characters develop and story lines unfold, always on the lookout for themes of redemption and sacrifice. Clint Eastwood's *Gran Torino* offers a rich portrait of selfless love; *Up in the Air* challenged me to consider the value of relationships and life's purpose.

The film *Comedian* follows the story of Jerry Seinfeld (post-television hit *Seinfeld*) as he creates an all-new stand-up act from scratch. Great comedians make comedy look easy, but as the film progresses, viewers get an inside look at the insecurities, self-doubts, and failures on stage. Appearances from Colin Quinn, Robert Klein, Ray Romano, Chris Rock, and Gary Shandling add insight and context to the world of comedy.

The film uncovers what every comedian knows: a single word makes the difference between a joke hitting or flopping. Seinfeld starts with a few minutes of awkward, uncomfortable material and develops it into a headline comedy act.

One scene from the film haunts me. Backstage, Seinfeld and newcomer Orny Adams discuss why someone chooses to be a comedian. Seeing his friends in more lucrative and stable professions, Orny second-guesses his decision. Seinfeld challenges him: no one becomes a comedian for the money or stability; they do it because they're created for comedy and so they'll be unsatisfied doing anything else.

I relate to Orny's doubts and fears. Like comedy, ministry isn't an easy profession. Other professions are far more lucrative and stable; but if you're created to serve, nothing else will do.

God often uses story in all of its forms to invite us deeper into his story. Though I believe God has a plan and purpose for each of us, *Simon Birch* allows me to see that truth lived out in a young boy's life. Though I struggle to wrap my mind around the concept of grace, I find comfort in the moment the priest gives Jean Valjean his freedom and silver candlesticks in *Les Misérables*.

As we read, watch, listen, and experience, God uses art to speak into our lives.

Nature

Most people who move to Colorado appreciate the outdoors. The mountains are vibrant with rock climbers, hikers, kayakers, skiers, snowboarders, and sports enthusiasts of all flavors. From my early childhood in Cocoa Beach, Florida, to my formative years in Steamboat Springs, Colorado, to my undergraduate years in Winston-Salem, North Carolina, I've always had a passion for outdoor activities.

Whether sailing or hiking, I'm in awe of the beauty of God's creation and the ways in which he reveals the sacred to us in nature. The power of God is emblazoned in everything from the Grand Tetons to the ladybug resting on a leaf. Hiking mountain peaks over 14,000 feet, elevations known as "fourteeners" in Colorado, I've mulled over what it means to persevere in the faith. Paddling a canoe on a choppy lake, I've pondered what it takes to find a spiritual balance. Outdoor landscapes invite us to experience the attributes of God and beckon us to pray.

Even the humblest offerings of nature can stir the hunger to speak and listen to God. My friend Dwayne describes watching a flock of geese flying overhead on an autumn morning. As he listened to their honking and watched their

V-shaped pattern, he noticed that the lead goose seemed to be putting forth more effort than the rest of the flock. Dwayne imagined the geese announcing to their leader "We are with you!" with each honk. When the leader of the flock smoothly dropped back, another strong-winged goose took the lead, and the former leader now enjoyed the draft of the flock. Watching the scene, Dwayne reflected on what it means to be a good leader—not just working hard and being out front, but also transitioning well into a follower.

God uses the wonders of nature to teach us valuable lessons and reveal the nature of the divine. Consider Adam and Eve in the garden. Not only did they experience perfect communion with God; they saw the wonders of his nature reflected in Eden, encountering God within the unblemished design. Even when the curtain closed on the garden, God didn't cut us off from glimpses of natural wonder and beauty. I gather hope from Romans 1:20: "For since the creation of the world His invisible attributes, His eternal power and divine nature, have been clearly seen, being understood through what has been made, so that they are without excuse." God's invisible qualities are still on display if we have eyes to see the wonder of creation.

I discovered this in-depth on a recent adventure, when I spent time with a shepherdess, a farmer, a beekeeper, and a vintner. With each of them, I opened the Scriptures and asked how they read various passages, not as theologians, but in light of what they do every day. Their answers changed the way I read the Bible. The travels became the foundation of my book *Scouting the Divine: My Search for God in Wine, Wool, & Wild Honey.*

Spending time with a shepherdess and her flock deepened my understanding of what it means for God to watch over us. Walking the fields with a farmer taught me about the seasons of life, patience, and fruitfulness. A beekeeper introduced me to the intricacies of a hive I never imagined existed. Insights into the work of a vintner shifted the way I view God's perspective of my life.

Years later I still find the Holy Spirit bringing to mind details of what I learned. At the winery in Napa Valley, California, we walked among the vines, inspecting each one. The vintner explained that after harvest, the vine is depleted of all nutrients and needs several months to heal after the last cutting. When the leaves begin to fall off and die, the vintner protects the vine from tractors, shears, and workers. If it doesn't have time to heal, production will drop the following year.

I recognize the parallels in my spiritual life. After seasons of high productivity, I need time to heal. Renewal doesn't happen in a few days or weeks, but requires a season of stillness, an intentional pulling away from the heavy demands of harvest to rest. In this place, which feels lonely and cold, God is still at work. My time with the vintner taught me not to despise the wintry seasons of my spiritual life, but to recognize that God is restoring and preparing.

God shares his wonder not only in what is said, but in how it's said. God cares about each of us and speaks into our lives in different ways. While some encounter the Lord through dreams and visions, others experience his voice through books or nature. The breadth of situations, circumstances, and methods God uses reminds us of the great effort he expends to reveal his love for each of us. May we pay attention to the multiple verbal and nonverbal cues God uses to garner our attention and stir our hunger to know him.

.006 Have You Heard?

A few years ago, Leif and I visited the Biltmore Estate in Asheville, North Carolina. We walked through the mansion and explored the grounds. When we checked into a hotel near the historic site, Leif discovered that BMW was hosting a special promotion, inviting people to take one of their new vehicles out for a spin on the Blue Ridge Parkway at no charge. We jumped at the opportunity.

Leif wears a size 14 shoe, but nowhere is his foot heavier than on the gas pedal. He drove through the tangled roads of the parkway at arrestable speeds. As the tires screeched around tight turns, I became grateful for the guardrails, which marked our course and kept us from flying off the edge of the mountain.

Just as metal guardrails help a leadfooted driver stay on the road, spiritual guardrails can help keep us on the path as we hear from God. These spiritual guardrails are questions we can ask ourselves to help us determine whether or not something is from God. Maybe you've been spending time with God—seeking, talking, listening. Perhaps you've had a dream, heard an internal audible voice, or felt an impression—but you've begun second-guessing. If you're not sure whether or not what you think you heard was God speaking to you, specific questions can act as guardrails for your spiritual journey.

The Bible serves as a bedrock, determining whether or not something is from God. If you feel led to do something that goes against the teachings of Jesus or the principles of Scripture, then what you're hearing isn't from God. That's why it's essential to ask, *Does what I heard line up with Scripture?*

A friend of mine became convinced that God was telling her to leave her husband so that she could be with another man. Once she married this man, she then claimed that God was going to use them as a couple to minister in powerful ways. My heart still breaks that she became so deluded as to believe that God was telling her to leave her husband, a man who, though imperfect, loved her much. The very things God speaks will ask us to love him and love others more, not less.

The Bible is the foundation and guide on hearing from God, but Scripture doesn't always speak to a specific situation. Should the next move be to New York or Los Angeles? Should the next job be at a small family business or a large corporation? Or is it time to launch a new business? Should one live on Oak or Elm Street? Marry Melinda or Melissa (assuming both are followers of Jesus)? We need other questions to determine whether or not what we heard is from God.

Another important question to consider is *Does what I heard line up with wise counsel?* Like many people, I've looked for mentors in my life who can provide wisdom concerning my finances, relationships, marriage, career, and faith. Over the years I've discovered that one mentor isn't enough. God speaks through a community. The person who may have the most wisdom in finances may be less adept in relationships. A marriage guru may not be as helpful when it comes to career choices. As a result, Leif and I have a short list of people we call based on the situation we're facing. All of them share common characteristics: they love God and long to see us grow in the fullness of who God created us to be; they pray for us; and they respond with honesty and grace, like my mom did when counseling me to give Leif a chance.

Godly counsel is invaluable. Proverbs 15:22 says, "Without consultation, plans are frustrated, but with many counselors they succeed."

Earlier this year I was considering taking on a project when one of my friends, who I consider a spiritual mentor, challenged me: "Every yes will cost you at least three nos. If you say yes to this, what three projects are you willing to reject?" Ouch! The question stung, but it also made me think. I began considering through prayer what my priorities were. What was God calling me to do, and what was a distraction? In the end, I turned the project down.

Another question I consider is, *Does what I heard leave me with a sense of peace?* In the excitement of hearing from God, I sense a wide range of emotions—surprise, joy, fear, awe, enthusiasm, sadness—that compel me toward a response. Before I act, I need to wait for peace. Called the "Prince of Peace," Jesus heralded peace in people's lives. Peace is a fruit of the Spirit and an attribute of God, a gift that acts as a guardrail in our lives, warning us when we're moving in the wrong direction. Philippians 4:7 promises, "The peace of God, which surpasses all comprehension, will guard *your hearts and your minds* in Christ Jesus" (emphasis added).

Last year, I was invited to be part of an event. As Leif and I prayed about the opportunity, we both lacked a sense of peace. Neither of us could identify the source of our unease; the people who invited us were dynamite, and their ministry reached thousands of people. But we chose to decline. Several months after the event, we discovered that a friend had accepted the invitation in our stead and contributed to its success, bringing a message of hope the people needed to hear at that time. We were grateful for our lack of peace, which had compelled us to decline the invitation, and opened the opportunity for our friend to be used by God to touch people's lives in a significant way.

One of the most important gauges is the question, *Is what I heard blanketed in love?* Love waters the shoots of humility and places the needs of others above our own. When we shine the light of 1 Corinthians 13 on what we think we've heard, we're better able to discern God's voice.

Everything I've ever heard from God compels me to love Jesus and others more. The nature of God's voice is that it calls us to maturity in love, nurturing the fruit of the spirit in our lives. If love is protecting our actions and decisions, then we'll be restrained from making grievous errors.

As much as I'd like God to tell me to eat more Godiva chocolate bars, God never has (and I doubt he ever will). Hearing from God requires us to step outside of ourselves. As humans, most of us cling to self-preservation and self-centeredness. God invites us to lay down our lives and live for something greater than ourselves. We need to ask, *Does what I heard increase my dependence on God?*

Much of what God calls us to do feels impossible. We lack the courage, the time, the resources, the relationships. Yet God still speaks and asks us to obey. In the process, we become more dependent—either God comes through or we fail.

We also need to ask, *Does what I heard line up with the vision, goals, and path of my life?*

Depending on what we think we've heard, we need to take a step back and consider the leading in the overall context of our lives. This is crucial for those with personalities (like mine) who get excited about all that God and his people are doing around the world. For example, my friend Shana launched a community development organization in Uganda known as Come Let's Dance, which is making an incredible difference in the lives of hundreds of African children.

Whenever Shana shares stories of transformed lives, I want to sell everything and move to Uganda. Before I post the "For Sale" sign in our front yard, though, I need to spend time in prayer and consider whether or not the desire is really from God. As I reflect on the vision, goals, and path God has established for me, I recognize that God created me to communicate. That's the journey I've been on since I was a young girl, and which continues to unfold today. Rather than pack my bags, I need to think about how I can use the talents and gifts I've been given to support my friend Shana: encouraging others to check out Come Let's Dance on my website and through my writing, supporting her through financial and physical gifts, and sharing the good news of her work with friends.

Sometimes God stretches us, inviting us into a new area or field, but even then we can usually identify how God has prepared us for such a moment. When we hear a whisper from God, especially one that offers a directive, we need to ask ourselves the other questions in the list and reflect on the work God has already done in our lives as well as what he has yet to do.

Stumbling Forward

Even after long bouts of prayer and consideration of all of these guardrail questions, we will make mistakes. We'll stumble over God's words, misinterpret and misinform. Learning to hear from God takes a lifetime.

When I lived in Colorado after college, I worked as a nanny for an incredible family with four children. The youngest was six months old when I started, and I watched him grow, take some of his first steps, and learn to communicate. His first attempts to speak were mumbled and jumbled. He'd make a sound and point at an object. As time passed, he progressed from one-syllable to two-syllable words— though even at age six he still called me Ma-gwit.

Just as it takes years to go from random sounds to grammatically correct sentences, it takes time to recognize, understand, and respond to God's voice in our lives. Along the way we can expect to make mistakes. First Corinthians

13:12 reminds us that we see as a poor reflection in a mirror. In antiquity, mirrors were made out of polished copper. The highest-quality copper mirrors failed to yield a clear image. Even on our best days, our understanding on this side of heaven is a bit fuzzy. Mistakes are inevitable. What's important is how we respond. Will we choose to grow discouraged and skeptical over the times God speaks, or learn and grow through them?

In 1997, I thought I was going to Israel. I prayed about Israel; my heart burned for it. Every time I turned on the news, I saw something on Israel. (Imagine that!) I felt that in my heart I heard, *Your feet will walk in the Holy Land*, and I was ready to buy a plane ticket. Somewhere along the line, I thought I heard (or really wanted to hear), *Your feet will walk in the Holy Land this year.* The year concluded and I never set foot in Israel.

Oops. Had God really spoken those words? I think God spoke some of them. I don't think he added the time frame *this year.* Either my own emotions or imagination added those words. Twelve years later, I traveled to Israel.

The experience taught me several lessons, including the importance of recording whatever I feel God is saying immediately. This prevents my emotions and imagination from polluting the whisper and morphing it into something it's not. I've also learned that whenever God is speaking something specific or date-related, I should be careful about whom I share the words with, so I don't end up looking silly or tarnishing the faith. We've all heard well-meaning people declare, "God told me …" or "God is going to …" and nothing happens. The claim doesn't pan out.

Rather than add to the list of abuses that come from people who claim to have heard from God, I've learned to follow the practice of Mary. God whispered to Jesus' mother many times about her special Son. Scripture records that Mary was overshadowed by the Most High. The angel Gabriel made a personal visit. Mary witnessed the miracles surrounding her relative Elizabeth when she became pregnant and gave birth to John the Baptist. And when Mary's son was born, wise men delivered gifts and strangers visited the humble stable. In the face of so much God activity and numerous whispers, Mary did something very wise: she "treasured all these things, pondering them in her heart."

Like the finest of dark chocolates, she knew that God's words are really morsels to be savored. Whenever God speaks something, we need to hold it in high regard. Keep it near our hearts. Let it roll over in our minds and spirits. The words God speaks are sacred and are often meant just for you.

I wish Israel was the only time I misheard from God, but

I've been wrong many times in my life. During my junior year of college, I wanted to study abroad in a Spanish-speaking country. I prayed and fasted, hoping for an insight into where to go. I looked at an atlas, studied foreign language programs, and spoke to my university's overseas guidance counselor. Then I discovered an inexpensive program in Salamanca, Spain, where I'd study Spanish, live with a family, and engage in the culture. The only problem was that my counselor refused to approve the program for credit. She approved other programs, but not the one I wanted to go on.

One night I went to the university's chapel and began praying. Flipping open the Bible, the page fell to Romans 15. I discovered the words that sealed my fate: "I plan to do so when I go to Spain." I couldn't believe my eyes! If the apostle Paul made a trip to Spain, then so could I! God was sending me to Spain to study abroad.

I kept reading just to make sure. Verse 28 reads, "I will go to Spain and visit you on the way." If that wasn't double confirmation, then I didn't know what was! My not-so-Christian attitude was "to heck with the guidance counselor"; after all, I had enough credits to graduate without her approval. I had heard from God.

In a few short months, I packed for an adventure in the country mentioned twice in Romans 15. Looking back,

I think they were ninety of the worst days of my life. Everything that could go wrong compounded and went horribly wrong. A riot broke out on my flight across the Atlantic. After the ruckus subdued, we learned that the plane had to be redirected through England for someone who needed a heart transplant. More than twenty hours later than scheduled, I arrived exhausted in Madrid. That's when I learned Spain's capital city has several train stations, but only one that travels to Salamanca. I didn't know enough Spanish to figure out which one.

Within an hour of arrival I was lost in downtown Madrid, carrying way too much luggage. Before I had left for Spain, I had purchased new boots, which now began cutting into the backs of my heels. I decided I was better off without, so I wandered around Madrid in bloody socks. Exhausted and frustrated, I sat down on the ledge of a fountain and cried. I also prayed, asking God to send someone, anyone, preferably an angel, to help me.

A young Spanish woman named Maria tapped me on the shoulder and asked me in broken English if I needed any assistance. She helped me find the train station, but by the time we arrived, the train had left. She drove me to the bus station and sent me on my way. An hour into the drive to Salamanca, the tire on the bus blew out, adding several hours to an already long trip. By the time I arrived at my hosts' home, I was exhausted, dirty, and in need of bandages.

That completed my first day in Spain.

The next eighty-nine were a lot like the first. My host family was horrible. (Yes, bad ones do exist, despite what college and overseas brochures promise.) The language school was even worse. I switched programs, which left me homeless for five days, living in a hotel during the transition. Everything I touched seemed to fall apart. I was scheduled to be on flights that were cancelled, buses that ran out of gas, and trains that broke down. I had a knack for picking the sketchiest youth hostels, and arriving at restaurants after they closed. My seventeen-year-old dog died when I was in Spain. A bird even pooped on me.

I matured a lot during my time abroad. I discovered God in ways only someone who has hit rock bottom and fallen even further knows the Lord. My survival skills were sharpened, and for the rest of my life, I will know how to find food, a hotel, and a bathroom in Spanish-speaking countries.

Now that the experience is years behind me I wonder, "Was the Lord really telling me to go to Spain?" Maybe. Maybe not. If he was asking me to go, I certainly wasn't asking God which program to choose. I selected the school and refused the wisdom of a guidance counselor. Ecclesiastes 8:5–6: "He who keeps a royal command experiences no trouble, for a wise heart knows the proper time and procedure. For there is a proper time and procedure for every delight." Looking back, I wish I had stumbled on *this* verse that fateful day in the chapel, rather than on the verses in Romans. Now whenever God whispers "go" to me, I am very careful to ask, "Where? How are we going to get there? Why are we going? What do you want us to do? What don't you want us to do?"

Though I still grimace when I think about Spain, I'm grateful for all I learned through the experience. I'd still rather be someone who tries to hear from God—even with the mistakes—than someone who never tries to listen and obey at all.

Learning to Fly

As a nine-year-old, Leo Tolstoy believed with all his heart that God had told him to fly. He was so confident that one day he jumped headfirst out of a third-story window. In one crashing moment, Tolstoy was introduced to his first big disappointment with God. Many years later, Tolstoy laughed at his youthful test of faith.

He survived the fall and so did his belief in God, but not everyone walks away from a leap of faith. Sometimes the injury is severe. Learning to hear and recognize God's voice isn't easy, and doesn't come without painful mistakes.

Years ago I was part of a fledgling community church whose members felt that God wanted to bring spiritual renewal and revival. Several of the members had specific dreams and visions that suggested God was about to move within this church in a profound way that would affect the surrounding area. Weeks rolled into months, then years. Growth stagnated. Then the news broke: the pastor was divorcing his wife because of an affair. The congregation divided. People left. The church deteriorated and still struggles today. Like others in the community, I had felt the rush of hope that God had spoken and was going to do something new in our church. Three years later, I felt disappointed and disillusioned. Now when I find myself hearing words of renewal or revival in other congregations, I have a hard time not being reminded of my negative experience.

Maybe you heard from God that a person was "the one." You knew in your spirit. You had absolute confidence. Everyone around you knew too; but the proposal was rejected, retracted, or never came to pass. Maybe you were given a vision of what God was going to do in your community, church, or ministry. You can still quote the words he spoke. But when you look around now, everything is a mess. The vision is gone. The dream is dead. Maybe you knew beyond a shadow of a doubt that God was going to heal someone, save someone, or repair a relationship. You prayed. You cried out to God. You poured out your tears, your very soul, and God answered you. You held the Scriptures, the words, the promise, in the palm of your hand. However, health keeps deteriorating. The person refuses to acknowledge God. There's no reconciliation.

And it hurts. It hurts deeply. You don't know if you even trust God now. After all, if God didn't come through on that issue, why trust the Lord will come through on the next one? Why should you believe God anymore? If he disappointed you once, what guarantees it won't happen again?

While those are all fair questions, if we focus on our disappointments, we will miss out on the divine appointments God has for us. If we're focused on what's gone awry, then we can't move forward into what God wants to do next.

As much as it hurts, God wants to heal and restore. I could offer a dozen guesses as to why things didn't work out as expected: maybe it wasn't really God speaking; maybe it wasn't his will. But they are all just guesses and seem pretty shallow in the depth of your pain. Besides, you've already played the situation through your mind at least a dozen times and know many of the possibilities yourself.

Sooner or later, you will have to choose to erase the memory of the disappointment and let God replace it with his love. Despite what may have happened, God is still true. God's promises remain valid. God's heart is still for you.

Here's a suggested prayer:

> God, _____ was such a disappointment. I need your forgiveness for any harbored hurt and I need your healing. Redeem the outcome of this situation for your glory. Pour your love and grace through everyone involved —including me. Strengthen my faith and draw my heart back to yours. In Jesus' name. Amen.

Though I've felt the bruises and carpet burns of clinging to things I thought were from God, but only left me disillusioned, none compare to the joy, delight, and wonder of discovering more of God, to the thrill of growing in my faith and experiencing him. Spiritual discoveries and instances when the *kairos* interrupts the *chronos* remind me of God's goodness and faithfulness. The times when I open the Scriptures and a passage comes alive are among my most precious treasures in this life.

When I look back on my mistakes, I'm still grateful for what God showed me through them. Though I was wrong about traveling to Israel years ago, I learned about the importance of keeping what God says between us until I'm confident that the words are from him. Through my wild trip to Spain, I discovered that I'm not designed to live overseas, and learned the need to honor those in authority. Through both experiences, I've grown and understood more about myself and God. Though it's not always easy, I wouldn't trade the adventure of knowing God's voice for anything.

Hungry Still

I'm convinced that people today know a lot more about how to *become* a Christian than about how to *be* one. Jesus says, "Behold, I stand at the door and knock; if anyone hears My voice and opens the door, I will come in to him and will dine with him, and he with Me." This verse isn't just an invitation to become a believer, but to live as one.

Notice that Jesus comes to the door empty-handed. He doesn't say, "Open the door and I'll give you a signed and sealed salvation card or a basket full of blessings." Though he takes on the image of a guest entering a home, he doesn't bring a housewarming gift—only himself.

Jesus isn't knocking to see what he can give or what he can get. He is knocking because he wants to share a deep relationship. How do we have depth? How do we anchor ourselves in the knowledge of God so that no matter what happens—whether the winds of prosperity or adversity blow—we remain faithful? By knowing God.

Living out that answer will cost everything, including

sacrifice and choosing the things of God over the things of this world. Wherever God's people are and whatever they're doing, God wants to take them one step further. If people already have a strong relationship with him, God wants to make it stronger.

Whenever God thinks of you, he has your best interests in mind; he has plans to take you further, deeper, and higher than you ever dreamed. This process begins when you seek God and spend time with him. Look for every opportunity to know God. Consider your daily schedule. What does it include? A workout at the gym? A trip to the post office? A lunch hour? A commute? Look for ways to include God in your activities. Invite God to accompany you by talking together. Look for moments—even if it's for only ten or twenty seconds—to steal away with him. God will reward your efforts as you reshape your inner life to be focused around him. As you seek God, you will find yourself abiding in him.

When Jesus spent time with his disciples, he provided a portrait of abiding. He ate meals with them, traveled with them, talked, laughed, and shared with them. Before Jesus expressed the importance of abiding in John 15, he lived the reality of abiding in front of their eyes. John 14:25: "These things I have spoken to you while abiding with you."

A favorite teacher once shared with me that during his

morning prayer time, he asked the Holy Spirit to stay with him. He heard the Holy Spirit respond, "Then don't leave me."

Our divine goal is to walk with God daily. Though I still stumble, I have discovered that listening to and obeying God is one of the richest aspects of life. Like the Israelites in the desert, I have found God's whispers to be like manna —something I need every day.

The Israelites didn't wake up in their tents with full stomachs every morning; they had to go out and gather the precious, life-giving bread. In the same way, I need to gather God's Word and wisdom for my life every day.

When I don't take time to be with God and listen, I start to lose my way. I lose sight of God's promises and intentions for my life. I begin focusing on the world and listening to its messaging instead. I find myself starving for God.

The whispers from God I've heard over the years have transformed the way I live and interact with the world. I've moved from having knowledge of God in my head to knowing him in my heart. I am not alone. Many of us are hungry for God's presence. We want to know and to make God known. If we are going to be God's people, part of the kingdom, then we must have more than information about God to offer; we must have God dwelling within us.

More information is available to us now than in the history of the world. Developments in numerous fields—scientific, historical, philosophical, and technological—result in new facts, statistics, quotes, and trends every day. Yet when most people ask questions about God, they aren't looking for information. If they were, they would go online or visit a library. They want to talk to someone who knows God.

Most people will choose to spend time with someone who has intimate knowledge of God over someone who simply knows some information about religion. People want to be around those who don't just know God's principles but who live them out and bear fruit through their faithfulness. God stands beside your desk at work, sits quietly in your kitchen, and waits for you in the pages of Scripture.

God is in the business of loving, maturing, and conforming us to the image of his Christ. Hearing from God was never meant to be kooky or spooky. Rather, God's voice directs, encourages, focuses, illuminates, and guides. If we are God's children, then as a good Father, God desires to spend time with us, communicate with us, and be with us —and we with him. We don't always have to hike through the desert to the burning bush, and we won't always turn around to find the angel of the Lord standing before us. Most often, we'll hear God's gentle whisper in the mundane moments and unexpected places.

May we become the people of God that we are intended to be by learning to hear and obey God's voice in the rhythms of the everyday. And may the hunger for God stir in your heart as you encounter the depths of his love for you.

Hidden Bonus Tracks

Hungry for God
Reflection & Discussion

These questions are designed to launch discussion among small groups and book clubs. Create some of your own. Add to the list. Engage as many people as you can in the responses.

Divine Appetite

1. What does it mean to you to hunger for God?

2. What types of situations or encounters stir your hunger for God and remind you of your need for him?

3. What types of situations or encounters make you feel the most distant from God?

4. Margaret describes spending months wondering, "Are you there, God?" Have you ever had a similar experience? Describe.

5. What do the following Scriptures reveal about fasting? Daniel 9; Psalm 35:13; Isaiah 58; Joel 2:15–16; Matthew 6:16–18; Matthew 9:14–15; Luke 2:36–37; Luke 18:9–14; 1 Corinthians 7:5.

6. If you've fasted in the past, what compelled you to fast?

7. How did fasting change you and your perspective of God?

8. Why is it important to look for God in the everyday experiences of life?

9. When have you discovered God in the everyday?

10. What compels you to want to hear God's voice more in your life?

.001 An Unforgettable Invitation

1. Margaret describes growing up seeing her mom read the Bible, but many people grow up without parents who pursue God. What image of knowing God did your parents instill? How has that image affected the way you understand God today?

2. If someone asked you how you hear from God, how would you respond? Try to explain your answer in such a way that it would not be confusing to someone new to their relationship with God.

3. Have you ever prayed and asked God for something that seemed outlandish that he provided? Describe.

4. Do you have an issue that you've wrestled with God in prayer? Describe.

5. Read 1 Kings 19. What surprises you most about this story?

6. What does this passage reveal about the way God speaks?

7. Read 2 Corinthians 12:7–10. Why do you think God allows us to experience thorns in life? In what ways do you find comfort in this passage?

8. Margaret writes, "Asking God to speak means that we must come to God on his terms, not our own." What are some of the terms or expectations that you approach God with in prayer? Do any of these expectations need to be reconsidered?

9. Why do you think our posture before God as we speak and listen is important?

10. How have you experienced God whispering into your life? How have you experienced a shout from God?

.002 Kairos Moments

1. Have you ever engaged in a game of Bible roulette by flipping open the Bible and reading whatever passage opened to you? What was the result?

2. Do you tend to celebrate more of the *chronos* or the *kairos* in life? Explain.

3. Read Genesis 6:13–21. How did God speak to Noah? What strikes you about what God said to Noah?

4. Read Genesis 12:1–3; 13:14–17; and 15:1–21. How did God speak to Abraham? Why do you think God didn't say everything he had to say to Abraham when first speaking to him in Genesis 12?

5. Read Genesis 21:11–21. Why did God speak to both Abraham and Hagar? What role did God's voice play in shaping each of their lives according to this passage? How would their stories be different if they had never heard God's voice?

6. Read Acts 9. Why did God speak to both Saul and Ananias? What role did God's voice play in shaping each of their lives according to this passage? How would their stories be different if they had never heard God's voice?

7. Why does God speak to you? What role does God's voice play in shaping your life? How would your story be different if you had never heard God's voice?

8. Have you ever experienced a Kairos Moment? Explain. What impact did the moment have on your faith?

9. Have you ever encountered something that seemed like a dead end that turned out to be a gift from God? Describe.

10. When have you discovered God in the everyday? Describe.

.003 Shaped by God's Voice

1. How would you describe the smell of the world that Jesus died for? Make a list of adjectives in the space below.

2. Margaret writes, "God can use what is spoken to others to help us recognize God's voice and presence in our lives." In what ways have you found this to be true in your own life?

3. Describe a recent experience when you felt God's conviction in your life. What was the result?

4. When was the last time you stumbled on a spiritual discovery while reading the Bible? How has the experience changed the way you think, feel, or understand God?

5. Margaret tells the story of the children distracted by the promise of donuts. What are some of the greatest distractions in your life?

6. It's been said that prayer doesn't change God as much as it changes us. In what ways do you agree or disagree with this statement?

7. In what ways do you feel challenged to "excel still more"?

8. Share the story of a time in your life when you experienced God's provision in a meaningful way.

9. Do you find stillness with God to be easy or challenging? Explain.

10. Margaret writes, "God's voice shapes us into works of grace and beauty." In what ways have you found this to be true in your own life?

.004 Readiness

1. How do you prepare yourself for attending church? Do you think preparing your heart and mind for church is important? Why or why not?

2. How do you seek God on a daily basis? What prevents you from seeking God more intentionally in your life?

3. Do you have a special location where you spend time with God? If so, describe.

4. What methods have you found to be most effective for studying and memorizing the Scriptures?

5. Do you feel comfortable asking God anything? Why or why not?

6. If you could ask God anything, what would you ask?

7. What do the following passages reveal about prayer and hearing from God? Jeremiah 7:23–24; Psalm 66:19; Proverbs 15:29; Isaiah 65:24; Matthew 7:7–8; John 6:44–45; John 10:1–5; Luke 18: 1–8; Romans 8:26; James 5:13.

8. When are you most likely to inquire of the Lord? When are you least likely to inquire of the Lord?

9. How might you take time to listen after talking to God through prayer? What is exciting and what is challenging about listening for God?

10. What roles do patience and obedience play in hearing from God? Which of these is more challenging for you?

.005 The Language of God

1. What are some of the most common ways God speaks to you?

2. Why do you think God uses so many ways to speak and reveal himself to different people?

3. Which of the ways that God speaks, listed in this chapter or beyond what is listed here, makes you feel the most comfortable? The most uncomfortable? Explain.

4. Are there any ways listed in this chapter you don't want God to use to speak to you, or that you especially wish he would? How do you think you'd respond if God spoke to you in that way?

5. Have you ever experienced a dream in which you felt God was speaking to you? Explain.

6. Do you find journaling an effective way for you to speak and listen to God? Why or why not?

7. What steps could you take to develop relationships with older, wiser mentors who can help you navigate life and your relationship with Jesus?

8. Read Psalm 65. What does the passage reveal about God's presence in nature?

9. What is one book, movie, or song that you felt God was using to speak to you?

10. In what ways have you experienced God's presence or voice through nature?

.006 Have You Heard?

1. Why do you think the most important question we can ask ourselves when we think we've heard from God is whether or not what we heard lines up with Scripture?

2. Of the six questions Margaret offers to reflect on in the process of discernment, which are you the most quick to ask? The most hesitant?

3. Why is peace essential in discerning God's voice in our life?

4. What do the following passages reveal about God's peace? Psalm 4:8; Proverbs 16:7; Isaiah 26:3; John 14:27; Ephesians 2:14; Philippians 4:7; 2 Thessalonians 3:16.

5. How do you respond when you encounter the silence of God?

6. Why do you think God is sometimes silent?

7. Describe an experience when you thought you had heard from God but were wrong. What was the result?

8. Have you ever been disappointed with God? What situation sparked the disappointment? What steps did you take to move beyond the disappointment?

9. Do you find comfort in knowing that we will all make mistakes when it comes to hearing God's voice? Why or why not?

10. How would you describe the process of learning to hear God's voice?

Hungry Still

1. British preacher Alexander Maclaren once observed, "We are able to have as much of God as we want. Christ puts the key to His treasure chest in our hands and invites us to take all we desire. If someone is allowed into a bank vault, told to help himself to the money, and leaves without one cent, whose fault is it if he remains poor? And whose fault is it that Christians usually have some meager portions of the free riches of God?"*

2. How has God's treasure chest of blessing been open to you? Have you accepted or refused the offer?

3. In Deuteronomy 6:3 (NIV), God commanded Moses with the opening words, "Hear, O Israel!" The same command followed in Deuteronomy 6:4; 9:1; 20:3; and 33:7. In Isaiah 51:7, God invites, "Listen to Me, you who know righteousness, a people in whose heart is My law." What steps are you taking to be more intentional about listening to God?

4. Do you believe God desires to speak to you? Why or why not?

5. Read John 13:23. What posture do you take when it comes to your relationship with Jesus? If you were dining with Jesus, what seat would you take at the table?

*L. B. Cowman, *Streams in the Desert* (Grand Rapids: Zondervan, 1997), 83.

6. "Hearing from God isn't designed for special people or only a select few. It's for every believer." In what ways do you agree with this statement? In what ways do you disagree?

7. How can you cultivate the hunger in your own life to know and love God more?

Behind the Scenes

Divine Appetite

Page 14: Judy Blume isn't the only one who can ask that question! For those who aren't familiar with it, Judy Blume's bestselling book *Are You There God? It's Me, Margaret* follows the adventures of a young girl who gets her first period. As a preteen, I was mortified by the title of the book. Now that I've grown older, I can't help but laugh every time I see this classic title on a shelf.

.001 An Unforgettable Invitation

Page 20: See Philippians 2:9–11 and Matthew 28:18–20.

Page 25: Exodus 3

Page 25: Deuteronomy 5

Page 25: Deuteronomy 1

Page 29: 2 Corinthians 12:7–10

.002 Kairos Moments

Page 36: Genesis 4:6–7

Page 36: Genesis 6:13–21

Page 36: Genesis 12:1–3

Page 36: Genesis 21:17

Page 36: Genesis 12:7

Page 36: Genesis 26:2–5, 24

Page 36: 1 Kings 3:5; 9:2

Page 36: Matthew 3:17

Page 37: Acts 9:4 NIV

Page 42: Matthew 10:30; Matthew 6:28; Matthew 6:26

Page 43: Genesis 1:1–2; Genesis 7; Exodus 2; James 5:17–18; Leviticus 15–16; Matthew 3:6–16; Revelation 22:1–2

.003 Shaped by God's Voice

Page 47: Jim Cymbala, *Fresh Wind, Fresh Fire* (Grand Rapids: Zondervan, 1997), 141–43.

Page 48: To learn more about the story of Scum of the Earth Church, check out their website at www.scumoftheearth.net. And you won't want to miss *Pure Scum: The Left-out, The Right-brained, and the Grace of God* by Mike Sares (Downers Grove, Ill.: InterVarsity, 2010).

Page 50: Adapted from Alice Gray, *Stories for the Heart* (Sisters, Ore.: Multnomah, 2001), 250–51.

Page 50: Jeremiah 18:4–6

Page 52: 2 Samuel 12:1–25

Page 54: John 16:8

Page 54: Hebrews 12:10–11

Page 59: Exodus 34:1–14

Page 59: 2 Kings 20

Page 61: Matthew 5:43–47

Page 62: Revelation 1:18 NIV, emphasis added

Page 63: NIV

Page 68: John 13:23

Page 69: James 4:2

Page 69: Matthew 9:20–22; Mark 5:25–34; Luke 8:43–47

.004 Readiness

Page 78: Psalm 63:1 NIV

Page 78: Deuteronomy 4:29

Page 80: www.redrocksonline.com

Page 81: Psalm 34:15

Page 84: If you have a good memory, then learn as many passages as possible; but if you struggle to memorize, then consider creative ways for the Scripture to thrive in your life.

Page 87: John 9:2

Page 88: Matthew 13:35

Page 88: 1 Corinthians 2:7

Page 93: *The Sacred Echo: Hearing from God in Every Area of Your Life,* a book and six-week Bible study, goes into depth into the repetitive nature of God's voice in our lives.

Page 95: NIV

Page 95: Acts 20:23–24 NIV

Page 96: Job 38–39

Page 100: Matthew 7:24–27

Page 101: Luke 18:22

.005 The Language of God

Page 105: Exodus 19:16–20

Page 106: Pronounced LEC-tsee-oh Di-VEE-nah

Page 106: Luke 2:19

Page 107: Luke 17:17–18

Page 112: John 14:16–18, 23

Page 115: "A Poet's Advice to Students" in e.e. cummings, a *Miscellany: A Miscellany,* ed. George James Firmage (New York: Argophile Press, 1958), 13.

Page 115: Isaiah 6:1; Daniel 2:28; Acts 9:11–18

Page 118: Luke 19:38 NIV

Page 118: Luke 19:40

Page 125: Bill shared the book where he found the story, and while the details are different in the original account, the message is the same. Gene Edwards, *The Inward Journey: The Road Towards Transformation* (Jacksonville, Fla.: SeedSowers, 1982), 17–19.

Page 127: Galatians 5:22–23

Page 130: Acts 13–14

Page 130: Acts 16–18

Page 131: To learn more about National Community Church, visit www.theater church.com.

Page 133: 2 Kings 2; Ruth 1–3; 1 Timothy and 2 Timothy

Page 134: Exodus 15

Page 134: 1 Chronicles 23:5

Page 134: Once every ten years, for example, the Passion Play is performed in Oberammergau, Germany, by villagers. The event began in 1633 and has become a centuries-old expression of Christian faith as well as a one-of-a-kind theatrical experience.

.006 Have You Heard?

Page 145: Isaiah 9:6

Page 145: Mark 5:34; Luke 7:50; Luke 8:48; Luke 10:5; Luke 24:36; John 14:27; John 16:33

Page 147: One constant need for Come Let's Dance is black shoes. In Uganda, children cannot attend school and receive an education without black shoes. Donations of children's black shoes are always welcome. In addition, Come Let's Dance refurbishes laptop computers for use by its youth. If you're interested in learning more about Come Let's Dance or meeting a need, check out www.comeletsdance.org.

Page 148: Stories abound of people being called to be missionaries in other no-name towns on the other side of the world. Some give compelling stories of how the last thing they ever wanted to do is live in a particular geographic zone or work in a certain profession, and yet that's where God called them. My friend Shannon, who hates deserts, served a Christian nonprofit in Israel a half a dozen years. Yet God's plan for most people's lives isn't *find out what they hate and then make them do it*. Psalm 37:4–6 promises, "Delight yourself in the Lord; and He will give you the desires of your heart. Commit your way to the Lord, trust also in Him, and He will do it. He will bring forth your righteousness as the light and your judgment as the noonday."

Hungry for God

Page 150: Luke 2:19

Page 151: Romans 15:24 NIV

Page 154: Philip Yancey, *Disappointment with God* (Grand Rapids: Zondervan, 1988), 77.

Page 157: Depending on the severity of your experience, I recommend *Where Is God When It Hurts?* and *Disappointment with God* by Philip Yancey. This gifted author asks tough questions about human suffering, disillusionment, and disappointment while reflecting on the faithfulness of God.

Hungry Still
Page 160: Revelation 3:20

Soundtrack

"The Transfiguration" *Seven Swans* by Sufjan Stevens
    (Sounds Familyre)

"Show Me What I'm Looking For" *Coming to Terms*
    by Carolina Liar (Atlantic)

"Gloria" *We Shall Not Be Shaken* by Matt Redman
    (Sparrow/Six Steps)

"Because of Your Love" *Heaven & Earth* by Phil Wickham
    (Ino/Columbia)

"You Cannot Lose My Love" *All Right Here* by Sara Groves
    (Ino/Epic)

"Everybody Hurts" *The Best of R.E.M* by R.E.M.
    (Warner Brothers)

"All Things New" *These Simple Truths* by Sidewalk Prophets
    (Word)

"God Speaking" *True Beauty* by Mandisa
    (Sparrow)

Props

Special thanks to ...

Mom and Dad, thank you for so many years of unending love and support. You have lived the Christian life as it was meant to be lived,with reckless abandon to Christ, an example and gift I will treasure forever.

An amazing team of friends provided feedback and suggestions, and pushed this book to be something more. Special thanks to Angela Scheff, editor extraordinare, for your wit and wisdom; Jana Reiss for your challenging and thought-provoking feedback. Winn Collier for encouraging me along the way; Cheri Johnson for adding literary flair but taming my outbursts; Jonathan Merritt for helping me weave the hungry theme and catch a glimpse of glaring blind spots; Chris Heuertz for not only broadening my writing skills but also the way I see the world; Jessica Ritchie for typing up this manuscript and rereading it multiple times, offering valuable insights and feedback; Kelly Johnson for creating beautiful work; Bill and Valerie Mangrum for their insight, guidance, and lovely Friday evenings together. Leif and I treasure you all!

Thank you for Chris & Christy Ferebee for their continued friendship and cheerleading. We're beyond grateful. Many thanks to Cheryl and Jim Clay who opened up their home and provided a much-needed writing getaway.

Thank you to the team at Zondervan. Tom Dean for going the extra mile as always, Curt Diepenhorst for being a rockstar, Sandy Vander Zicht for diving into transition and the unknown, and Becky Philpott for her editing prowess. A shout-out goes to Dudley Delffs for making this project possible.

And thank you to my readers, some of whom have been traveling with me for over a decade since *God Whispers* first released, and to my new friends who have joined me for more recent books, I'm grateful. You are the reason I write. Thanks for continuing the spiritual adventure—I look forward to many more miles together.

Fall in love with God all over again.

Imagine what it would look like to have an organic relationship with God—one that is stripped of all pollutants and additives of this world. *The Organic God* removes the unhealthy fillers and purifies our relationship with the God of the Scriptures. Through personal stories and scriptural insights, Margaret Feinberg shares glimpses of God's character—big-hearted, kind, beautiful, mysterious—that point you to an authentic and naturally spiritual relationship with him, allowing you to truly discover God in a healthy, refreshing new way. You won't be able to help but fall in love all over again.

Also available in e-book and audio download formats.

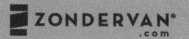

The Sacred Echo 6-Session DVD Bible Study

The Sacred Echo **Bible study** is a 6-session DVD study designed to help participants develop a more vibrant prayer life and recognize the repetitive nature of God's voice in their lives.

To receive a FREE DVD sampler of *The Sacred Echo* and other DVD Bible studies, simply email **sampler@margaretfeinberg.com**. We'll get one in the mail to you.

Visit **margaretfeinberg.com/store** to order.

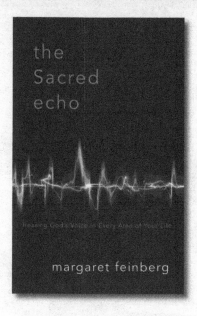

Scouting the Divine 6-Session DVD Bible Study

Scouting the Divine **Bible study** is a 6-session DVD study in which Margaret spends time with a shepherd, beekeeper, farmer, and vintner in order to unlock the beauty and wonder of Scripture. Fresh and insightful, you won't read the Bible the same way again.

To receive a FREE DVD sampler of *Scouting the Divine* and other DVD Bible studies, simply email **sampler@margaretfeinberg.com**. We'll get one in the mail to you.

Visit **margaretfeinberg.com/store** to order.

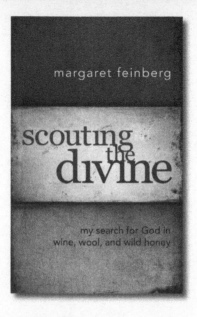

Connection

Authentic. Genuine. Winsome.

A popular speaker at churches and leading conferences such as Catalyst and Thrive, Margaret Feinberg was recently named one of the "30 Emerging Voices" who will help lead the church in the next decade by *Charisma* magazine and one of the "40 Under 40" who will shape Christian publishing by *Christian Retailing*. She has written more than two dozen books and Bible studies including the critically acclaimed *The Organic God, The Sacred Echo, Scouting the Divine* (Zondervan), and their corresponding DVD Bible studies. She is known for her relational teaching style and inviting people to discover the relevance of God and his Word in a modern world.

Margaret and her books have been covered by national media including CNN, the Associated Press, *Los Angeles Times*, *Dallas Morning News*, *Washington Post*, *Chicago Tribune*, *Denver Rocky Mountain News*, *Newsday*, *Houston Chronicle*, Beliefnet.com, Salon.com, USATODAY.com, MSNBC.com, RealClearPolitics.com, Forbes.com, and many others.

Margaret currently lives in Morrison, Colorado, with her 6'8" husband, Leif. When she's not writing or traveling, she enjoys anything outdoors, lots of laughter, and their superpup, Hershey. But she says some of her best moments are spent communicating with her readers. So go ahead, become her friend on Facebook or follow her on twitter: @mafeinberg.

You can drop her a line at:

Margaret Feinberg
PO Box 441
Morrison, Colorado 80465

Margaret@margaretfeinberg.com

www.margaretfeinberg.com

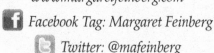 *Facebook Tag: Margaret Feinberg*

Twitter: @mafeinberg

Share Your Thoughts

With the Author: Your comments will be forwarded to the author when you send them to *zauthor@zondervan.com*.

With Zondervan: Submit your review of this book by writing to *zreview@zondervan.com*.

Free Online Resources at
www.zondervan.com

Zondervan AuthorTracker: Be notified whenever your favorite authors publish new books, go on tour, or post an update about what's happening in their lives at www.zondervan.com/authortracker.

Daily Bible Verses and Devotions: Enrich your life with daily Bible verses or devotions that help you start every morning focused on God. Visit www.zondervan.com/newsletters.

Free Email Publications: Sign up for newsletters on Christian living, academic resources, church ministry, fiction, children's resources, and more. Visit www.zondervan.com/newsletters.

Zondervan Bible Search: Find and compare Bible passages in a variety of translations at www.zondervanbiblesearch.com.

Other Benefits: Register yourself to receive online benefits like coupons and special offers, or to participate in research.

ZONDERVAN.com/
AUTHORTRACKER
follow your favorite authors